THE BIOGRAPHY OF GENERAL OF THE ARMY, DOUGLAS
MACARTHUR

THE BIOGRAPHY OF GENERAL OF THE ARMY, DOUGLAS
MACARTHUR

S. L. MAYER

63796

GALLERY BOOKS
An Imprint of W. H. Smith Publishers Inc.
112 Madison Avenue
New York City 10016

Published by Gallery Books
Distributed by W.H. Smith Publishers Inc.
112 Madison Avenue
New York, New York 10016

Produced by
Bison Books
17 Sherwood Place
Greenwich
Connecticut 06830, USA

ISBN 0-8317-5793-0

Printed in Hong Kong

Reprinted 1983

Main Line)
June 1984
1540

CONTENTS

1:THE YOUNG WARRIOR   6
2:BETWEEN THE WARS   16
3:THE WARRIOR DEFEATED   38
4:THE WARRIOR RETURNS   66
5:THE WARRIOR SHOGUN   87
6:THE WARRIOR UNLEASHED   120
7:OLD SOLDIERS NEVER DIE...   138
INDEX   167

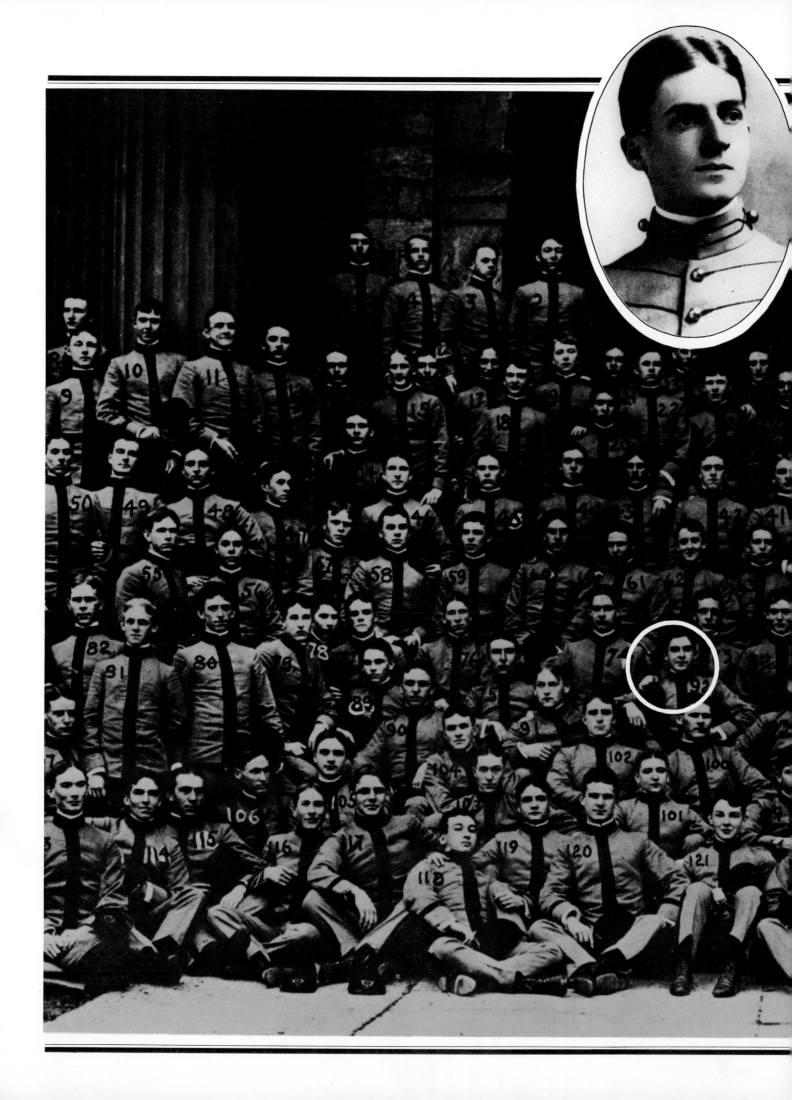

1: THE YOUNG WARRIOR

Douglas MacArthur's boyhood ideal was his father, not unlike most boys, but in Douglas's case he had a lot to live up to. Arthur MacArthur's life as a soldier covered almost a half-century of American military history, beginning with the Civil War, through the Indian wars, and up to and including the Spanish-American War. Arthur MacArthur was 15 when the Civil War broke out, and he was recommended to Abraham Lincoln for entry into the United States Military Academy at West Point. Since all vacancies had been filled, Arthur obtained a commission in the 24th Wisconsin Volunteers, one of the most illustrious units ever to fight for the Union. General Sheridan gave him special commendation at the Battles of Perryville and Murfreesboro, and after having contracted typhoid which kept him out of action for a time, he returned to his regiment to fight under Sheridan at Missionary Ridge, putting the Confederates of General Bragg to rout. The regiment voted MacArthur the rank of major on the spot and he was given command soon afterward.

He was 19 years old. Wounded on two occasions thereafter, and subsequently voted the Congressional Medal of Honor, the highest decoration any American soldier can win, Colonel MacArthur was demobilized at the end of the war, but obtained a commission in the regular army, which was to be reduced to a puny 54,000 in 1866.

This small army fought the Indians in various campaigns, and Arthur MacArthur served in many of them in the seven years he fought on the western frontier. Posted to New Orleans in 1875, he met and married Mary Pinckney Hardy, a girl descended from an old Virginia family, and whose brothers fought for the Confederacy. The couple had three children: Arthur, born in 1876; Malcolm, born in 1878, who died as a child; and Douglas, who was born at the Arsenal Barracks in Little Rock,

Arkansas, on 26 January 1880. When Douglas was four the family moved to an army base near the Mexican border, and there he was taught to ride and shoot even before he could read or write, as MacArthur relates in his *Reminiscences*. He recalled that his mother taught him his first principles, among them . . . 'a sense of obligation. We were to do what was right no matter what the personal sacrifice might be. Our country was always to come first.'

Douglas was educated in various places throughout the 1880s and 1890s, wherever his father was assigned. By 1897 Colonel MacArthur was transferred to St Paul, Minnesota and it was decided that Douglas should study for a competitive examination to be held in May 1898 for a vacancy at West Point, nominated by a Congressman from Milwaukee. He came first in the exams and went to the Point in June 1899.

By that time the Spanish-American War had broken out and had been won, in spite of the fact that the American army had dwindled to less than 25,000 while the Spanish army in Cuba alone had many times that number. Congress voted for a wartime increase in the army's strength, and several ill-organized landings were made on Cuba. At the same time Commodore Dewey's naval forces had won an overwhelming victory over the Spanish at Manila Bay. Soon after this victory three brigades landed to occupy the capital of the Philippines and its environs, one of them led by Brigadier General Arthur MacArthur. The long involvement of the United States and the MacArthur family in Philippine history had begun.

In the mopping-up operations against the Philippine nationalist leader, Aguinaldo, which were far more considerable than the American effort to 'liberate' the Filipinos from Spanish rule, Arthur MacArthur played a vigorous role. By the end of 1899, after Douglas had entered West Point, there were over 50,000 Americans in the field against the Philippine nationalists, and Arthur MacArthur was one of the most important leaders of the American attack. By June 1900 Arthur MacArthur had succeeded

Inset left: MacArthur at West Point.
Left: MacArthur (encircled) with the members of the West Point Class of 1903.

General Otis as commander of the American contingent and as governor-general of the Philippines, and by now even more stringent measures were taken against the insurrectionists.

By July the resistance on Luzon, the main island of the Philippine group, had begun to collapse, and although guerrilla warfare continued sporadically for almost a decade, the back of the resistance had been broken. Arthur MacArthur was succeeded as civil governor by William Howard Taft, later to become President of the United States and subsequently Chief Justice, the only American ever to have served in the two highest offices of his country. Arthur MacArthur returned to take an appointment at home.

By this time Douglas MacArthur had spent a year at the Point. By the standards of the day, which were by no means lax, discipline at the Point was very strict. At the turn of the century hazing, or bullying, of the 'plebes' (first-year men) by senior classmates, which still goes on but which is very mild compared to what once existed, became a subject of a Congressional investigation. During his second year at the Point young Douglas MacArthur was called before the court as a principal witness in a case in which he had been an alleged victim. MacArthur was asked to name the upperclassmen involved in the incident. Overcome by a feeling of nausea, he pleaded for mercy but refused to name the offenders. He expected to be placed under arrest after he had been taken to quarters once the ordeal was over. Sixty years later he recalled waiting 'for that dread step of the adjutant coming to put me under arrest. But it never came. The names were obtained through other means. . . .'

With his father gaining a certain amount of publicity for his part in the Philippine operations, MacArthur, even at this time a young man who felt the heavy weight of tradition and pride in his family's honor, worked diligently to reach the top of his class in three of the four years he spent at West Point, which included being first in the corps during his final year. He had played on the baseball team during two of those years. He was perhaps the most handsome, most photogenic cadet at the Point and was popular with the girls, not only for those reasons, but also because he was

Above: US forces during the suppression of the Philippine uprising. Arthur MacArthur, Douglas' father, in front row, center.

the son of Arthur MacArthur. One biographer mentions an incident in which he was asked by a wide-eyed girl if he really were the son of General MacArthur. He replied, 'Yes'm, General MacArthur has that proud distinction.' There are no records kept at West Point for the most modest man in MacArthur's class, but it probably can be safely said that Douglas did not come first in that category.

In June 1903 MacArthur was commissioned as a second lieutenant in the engineers, at that time an élite corps of the American army, and was sent to the Philippines, two years after his father had been sent home and who now, incidentally, was stationed on the Pacific Coast. Returning to California after a year overseas, Douglas later joined his father as an aide-de-camp in Japan when Arthur MacArthur was sent there to report on the Russo-Japanese War. Both were subsequently instructed to make a tour of Southeast Asia and India. They travelled and talked to leading figures in Hong Kong, Singapore, the Dutch East Indies, Ceylon and India. The son remarked in his memoirs that this experience 'was without doubt the most important factor in my entire life. It was crystal clear to me that the future and, indeed, the very existence of America, were irrevocably entwined with Asia and its island outposts.' It was an opinion that MacArthur was to retain throughout his life.

In 1908 Douglas MacArthur graduated from the Engineer School of Application and during this period served as ADC to President Theodore Roosevelt. His father's career after the great Asian tour took a turn for the worse, however. Now a lieutenant general, it was expected that he would be in line for an appointment as Chief of Staff, but during Roosevelt's second administration William Howard Taft, with whom the elder MacArthur had clashed in the Philippines, was Secretary of War, and this may well have hurt his chances for advancement.

Arthur MacArthur retired in June 1909, just a few months after Taft had taken the oath of office as the successor to President Roosevelt. Three years later he fell dead while addressing the 50th reunion of his old Civil War regiment. He had been ill and had sent his regrets that he would be unable to attend the reunion, but the governor of Wisconsin and the two senators from that state had cancelled their engagement there as well because of the extreme heat. In this last reunion of the famous 24th Wisconsin Regiment the organizers begged their old commander to attend anyway. When the toastmaster called upon Arthur MacArthur to speak, he began by recalling the old

Right: An American bivouac in Mindanao, southern Philippines, circa 1905.

Above right: US Marines on a search and destroy mission near Olongapo, in the Philippines around 1903–04.

Left: The young MacArthur at work as a censor in the War Department in 1917.

triumphs. Then he faltered and collapsed, and the regimental surgeon rushed to his side. He turned to the audience and simply said, 'Comrades, the General is dying.' In the middle of the room the chaplain began to repeat the Lord's Prayer, and the 90 odd men came to the side of their old commander and joined in. The battle flag was wrapped around his body. Douglas MacArthur recalled that incident with reverence. Perhaps his melodramatic account of the occasion of his father's death was somewhat exaggerated; perhaps his emotional remark that 'the world changed that night; never have I been able to heal the wound in my heart' was exaggerated too. His sense of tradition, of duty to his family and his country were exceptional. It is enough to say that he admired his father tremendously and envied his reputation. Even at this stage in his life his chief desire was to live up to his father's name and to surpass it. His father's lack of political subtlety, as illustrated by his alienation of Taft, was another characteristic, as well as personal courage and forthrightness, which Douglas MacArthur was to inherit from his father.

Following his father's death MacArthur, by now a well-travelled young man with rich experiences behind him, still lacked extensive regimental and staff experience. He left his temporary posting at Fort Leavenworth in Kansas, where he met George C Marshall, who had passed the Staff College there, and went to Washington as a member of the Engineer Board. While on the Board he was able to arrange a trip to the Panama Canal Zone, where he was brought in on the last stage of the construction of the canal.

In 1911 MacArthur received some valuable experience from Leonard Wood, the Chief of Staff, by working with him on military exercises in Texas, which were meant as a show of strength to the Mexicans across the border, whose revolution was beginning to make both the Mexican land-owning classes and the American government nervous. Partially as a reward for this operation, MacArthur was posted to the general staff in Washington in 1913. Only a few months after this appointment he was able to see his first active service when the United States intervened in the Mexican Revolution. MacArthur was sent by Wood to Vera Cruz to observe and report after the marines had landed there on a pretext. MacArthur had instructions that if fighting broke out between the occupying American force of over 7000 US Army and Marine Corps personnel and the Mexican army he was to join the staff of a field army operating out of Vera Cruz under the command of Wood himself. MacArthur distinguished himself in Mexico, and war was avoided. MacArthur returned to Washington and in 1915 was appointed major.

America began to build up her armed forces during the so-called preparedness campaign, anticipating not only active participation in World War I, which had broken out in Europe, but possible intervention along the Mexican frontier, where most of the United States armed forces were stationed during the more active phase of the Mexican Revolution as well as the Pancho Villa raids across into New Mexico, which General Pershing punished by invading northern Mexico with a rather large raiding party. Tension along the frontier was high, therefore, when the United States severed diplomatic relations with Germany in February 1917.

The Zimmermann Note, which rallied Western and Southwestern American public opinion behind President Wilson, made a two-front war a very real possibility for the United States. A naval war against Germany combined with an American Expeditionary Force to France as well as a border war with the Mexicans would have hindered American military success both in Europe and in Mexico; American armed forces were simply too weak to cope. For that reason Woodrow Wilson took steps to introduce a Conscription Bill, the first attempt made in that direction since the Civil War. After war had been declared against Germany in April, a Selective Service Act had been drafted and passed through Congress. The aim of the act was to raise an army of half a million men to send to France as soon as possible as well as an additional and substantial reserve force within the United States. These early estimates, which at the time sounded high, were more than met and greatly surpassed before America's 20-month long participation in World War I was over.

General Funston was expected to lead the American Expeditionary Force in France, but he died in February 1917, and it was left to Douglas MacArthur to carry the news to President Wilson. In May his replacement was appointed: General John J (Black Jack) Pershing. He set up his headquarters in France to prepare for the hundreds of thousands of Americans who were expected to pour into Europe by the autumn of 1917, and hopefully, the spring of 1918. The Allies were sorely in need of fresh troops; millions of lives had already been lost on both sides of the Western Front and by mid-1917 the Allied cause was considerably weakened. Both Britain and France urged the Americans to come quickly.

Right: Major MacArthur in a characteristic pose with corn-cob pipe at San Antonio, Texas, during the border fighting with Mexico in 1916.
Below: Fighting in the remains of the St Mihiel wood on the Western Front in the summer of 1918. The presence of American troops saved the Allied cause in World War I. By 1918 the manpower of the other Allied nations was nearly exhausted while the German forces on the Western Front were being strengthened by troops drawn from Russia.

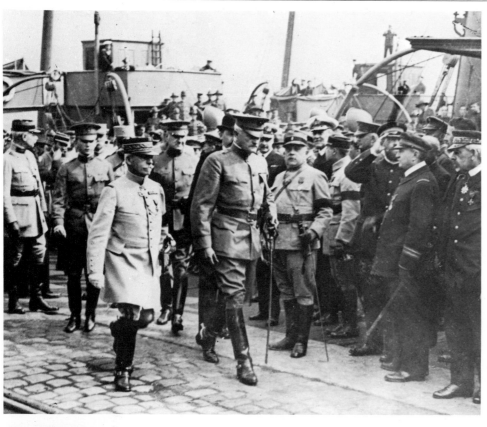

By the end of 1917 only 175,000 Americans had arrived and only four of the 24 divisions Pershing promised the Allies were complete. MacArthur, who had met Pershing soon after he graduated from West Point, and who was impressed by his soldierly bearing and strength of character, was assigned to the Rainbow Division, a unit so called because it drew its members from all parts of the United States rather than from a territorial or state unit, a virtual tradition in the American armed services now, but an innovation at that time. It was one of the first American units to enter the fighting in France and became

Left: General John J (Black Jack) Pershing arrives in Boulogne to organize the American Expeditionary Force in June 1917. His group of three men became more than a million within one year.
Below: Memorial Day services at Baccarat, France in May 1918. MacArthur is the third American from the left behind French Lt Gen Duport. Also present Maj Gen Mencher and Brig Lenihan.

one of its most illustrious divisions. MacArthur landed with the Rainbow Division at St Nazaire in October 1917, and it was soon sent to the Meuse Valley to continue its training. Both American and Allied officers recognized the fact that the American units were under-equipped and under-staffed as well as under-prepared, and it was accepted reluctantly on all sides that it would take time before any American unit was battle-ready. The Rainbow Division was one of the first to be prepared. It moved up to the Front along the Luné-ville-Baccarat area in February 1918, to relieve a French unit. In his first action MacArthur distinguished himself by leading a raiding party through the barbed wire. For this action MacArthur received not only the American Silver

Below: MacArthur with French General de Bazelaire watching maneuvers of the 42nd (Rainbow) Division near Glonville in early July 1918.

Star but the Croix de Guerre, which General de Bazelaire pinned on his tunic and then kissed him on both cheeks.

Once the Rainbow Division was ready for the attack in March, MacArthur was decorated with the Distinguished Service Cross, a battle decoration second only to the Congressional Medal of Honor, when he led a raiding party into German lines. It was typical of the kind of soldier MacArthur was: courageous but also determined to create a heroic image for himself, perhaps to satisfy his own vanity, partly perhaps to live up to the reputation of his father; but certainly to impress others around him as well. MacArthur admitted as much in his memoirs. When he later received a second Distinguished Service Cross, MacArthur remarked that the citation 'more than satisfied my martial vanity.' It would be imprudent to characterize MacArthur as merely a vain man. He was learning the art of war and was to become a master of it. He was especially

impressed by defense-in-depth tactics, in which the forward trenches were held by a light picket line and the main strength held back ready to surprise and destroy the enemy attack.

In July, as the Allies were being pushed back in Germany's last great offensive of the war, MacArthur was in the thick of the fighting, usually leading his men into battle, and when, on the 19th, the beleaguered Rainbow Division was withdrawn after having suffered over 1500 casualties, he was awarded his second Silver Star. Once the German thrust had been halted, the Allies began a counteroffensive almost immediately, and after only five days' rest, the Rainbow Division was again thrown into battle. Relieving the weary 26th Division, the 42nd (Rainbow) entered the Marne salient on 25 July and began to drive the enemy back. MacArthur compared the tactics used at this point with the tactics seen in the Indian wars in the Western United States. 'Crawling forward in

Above: Enthusiastic American troops on the way to the Western Front in the summer of 1918.

twos and threes against each stubborn nest of enemy guns,' he wrote, 'we closed in with the bayonet and hand grenade. It was savage and there was no quarter asked or given. It seemed to be endless. Bitterly, brutally the action seesawed back and forth.' MacArthur lived up to his heroic words. Moving inexorably forward after almost nonstop fighting for four days, MacArthur, exhausted, fell asleep. The division was again withdrawn into the reserve on 2 August after having suffered over 5500 casualties in its costliest battle. MacArthur was made a Commander of the Legion of Honor and given a second Croix de Guerre as well as yet another Silver Star to add to his collection.

By the time the Germans, themselves exhausted, with their supplies and personnel woefully depleted, had withdrawn to the Hindenburg Line, Pershing, tasting triumph, now realized his great ambition: to lead an offensive with the newly formed First American Army aimed at the St Mihiel salient. The main attack was to be made by the American I

Corps (four divisions) and the IV Corps (three divisions, including MacArthur's 42nd). The salient had existed since 1914 and was 18 miles across and 13 miles deep. Behind the front line lay a second position and across the base a third, which was part of the Hindenburg Line and consisted of wire and many concrete posts. The Germans were ready to withdraw to this seemingly impregnable line. When the infantry advanced against the line MacArthur was with the forward troops of his brigade. Within five days the salient had been eliminated and the enemy was retreating in what Pershing described as 'considerable disorder.' Almost 16,000 prisoners had been taken with 450 guns. The 42nd Division lost 1207 men, and the First Army's casualties were about 7000. Brigadier General MacArthur was again awarded two more Silver Stars.

The Rainbow Division was once more withdrawn to prepare for its next offensive: the Meuse-Argonne. As veteran divisions like the 42nd needed rest, Pershing did not plan to use them in the first phase of the offensive, which extended over (eventually) an 80-mile front and which was to last 47 days. The 42nd entered the fighting on 11 October.

MacArthur organized an enveloping attack which proved successful, after which he was promoted to major general and awarded his second Distinguished Service Cross. Withdrawn from the fighting again, the 42nd returned to the Front on the extreme left of the American armies on 5 November, after an incident in which MacArthur, with some of his forward troops, was stopped by American troops of another Corps. Once the muddle was sorted out, both American and French forces pushed forward against the enemy in their attempt to take Sedan, but were pushed back by heavy fire. On the night of 9–10 November, the 42nd Division was withdrawn, MacArthur was awarded his seventh Silver Star, and the next day the Armistice ending the war came into effect at 11.00.

There were those who were jealous of MacArthur's many awards, some more of which were to come his way, including a number of foreign decorations as well as the Distinguished Service Medal. MacArthur's idiosyncratic methods were even the subject of a brief and fruitless investigation. For example, he failed to wear a helmet or carry a gas mask, and in fact was hospitalized after the war with a serious throat infection which, he claimed, occurred because he had taken too much gas on the front. He also had a habit of going unarmed and refusing to lead from the rear, which, although dangerous, was ultimately to his credit. When Pershing was informed of this investigation, he was reported to have replied: 'Stop all this nonsense.

Below: Brig General MacArthur in a grandiloquent mood in Sept 1918 occupying the chair of the lord of the Chateau St Benoit.

Above: MacArthur receives the Distinguished Service Medal from Pershing in Remagen, Germany in 1919. By then he was already America's most highly decorated soldier.

MacArthur is the greatest leader of troops we have, and I intend to make him a division commander.' The Armistice prevented his promotion, however, since Washington ordered that advancement of generals must cease once the Armistice came into force.

Despite the heavy casualties suffered by the Rainbow Division, it achieved wide acclaim and so did MacArthur. His superior officer wrote in a letter to Pershing that MacArthur had 'actually commanded larger bodies of troops on the battleline than any officer in our army, with, in each instance, conspicuous success.' He had 'filled each day with a loyal and intelligent application to duty such as is, among officers in the field and in actual contact with battle, without parallel in our army.' There can be no doubt about the fact that, at 38 years old, MacArthur had proved beyond any shadow of doubt his merit as a soldier and as a leader of men, praised by his inferiors and superiors alike. No wonder some of the boys down at HQ were jealous. Despite the remarks of recent historians who have tried to revise MacArthur's grandiose opinion of himself, his World War I record leaves no doubt: he was a great soldier and deserved the high acclaim that his country and her Allies chose to bestow upon him.

2:BETWEEN THE WARS

MacArthur's Rainbow Division was one of the nine American divisions which took part in the occupation of the Rhineland after the Armistice. Although ill during the first months of 1919, MacArthur enjoyed the days of rest and relaxation so welcome to one who had endured so much. His admiration for the German people and their well-ordered way of life, as he later put it, as well as their thrift and geniality impressed him tremendously. He remarked that the boastful and arrogant feeling that he and the men shared toward the Germans at the end of the war was soon replaced by a 'realization of the inherent dignity and stature of the great German nation.' The well-known Kansas journalist, William Allen White, visited him in January 1919 in his house overlooking the Rhine. He was enthralled by MacArthur, and White was not one to be easily impressed, having known on personal terms almost everyone who was anyone in Washington for many years. Yet he remarked that he 'had never before met so vivid, so captivating, so magnetic a man. He was all that Barrymore and John Drew hoped to be. . . . His staff adored him, his men worshipped him, and he seemed to be entirely without vanity.' But MacArthur was a great actor.

Reluctantly he left for home in April, and MacArthur enjoyed a relaxing crossing on the *Leviathan*, occupying a 5000 dollar suite which consisted of four rooms and three baths. He regretfully remarked that although he reached New York on 25 April, 'where-oh-where was that welcome they told us of? Where was that howling mob to proclaim us monarchs of all we surveyed? Where were those bright eyes, slim ankles that had been kidding us in our dreams? Nothing – nothing like that. One little urchin asked us who we were and when we said – we are the famous 42nd – he asked if we had been to France. Amid a silence that hurt – with no one, not even the children to see us – we marched off the dock!'

Left: MacArthur (top left) with fellow officers in the American Army of Occupation in the Rhineland in 1919.

MacArthur's welcome in Washington was somewhat warmer, if not exultant. He was summoned to the Office of the Chief of Staff, Peyton C March, and told he had been appointed Superintendent of West Point. He took command there in June. While others who had distinguished themselves in the war were not promoted and even lost their wartime rank, like George S Patton, George C Marshall, and Joseph W Stilwell, MacArthur retained his wartime rank of brigadier general. Furthermore, he was one of the youngest men ever to become Superintendent of the Point. His immediate predecessor was 71; MacArthur was 39. He had been informed that the Point was 40 years behind the times, and immediately set about the task of modernizing the educational system there. Only two of the professors had university degrees; almost all the others were graduates of West Point with little or no civil education. Normally the teaching officers would stay at the Point for four years, teach as best they could without any previous formal training, and then return to a military assignment.

MacArthur recognized immediately that modern war would be fought by nations in arms, not merely small professional armies, and that these conditions would demand officers who had a broad, liberal education rather than training merely in the arts of war. MacArthur introduced a broader curriculum, brought in university lecturers to teach the cadets, and sent members of his own teaching staff to visit other colleges and universities. Many of the social abuses which members of his generation suffered at the hands of senior cadets were abolished, and compulsory participation in team games was introduced to improve *esprit de corps* and to make certain that all cadets, especially ones not adept in athletics, would be competent to supervise games once in the service. Cadets were sent to regular army units for two months during the summer to bring them into contact with real army life in contrast with the secluded and somewhat spoiled atmosphere which West Point had created in the past.

Above: MacArthur with the Chief of Staff of his Rainbow Division, Walter B Wolf, during the occupation of the Rhineland in 1919.

Resistance to these changes came, of course, from some members of the staff and old graduates, but MacArthur won the support of many of the officers who were closest to him, and in the end West Point had gone through the most serious reforms since the time of Sylvanus Thayer soon after the founding of the academy at the turn of the 19th century.

In his three years at the Point MacArthur, with the help of the National Defense Act of 1920, helped put the academy into the 20th century. The army, however, soon fell into disrepair. Demobilization and the desire of the nation to return to a peacetime basis, 'normalcy,' as President Harding called it, were natural enough reactions of an America which had become disillusioned with European diplomacy after the failure of the Congress to ratify the Treaty of Versailles or to join the League of Nations. Despite the protests of Pershing, who had become Chief of Staff in 1921, the army was reduced to 175,000 men, with only 12,000 officers, an improvement, perhaps, on the stan-

dards maintained before World War I, but a level inconsistent with America's increased responsibilities and interests in the world outside the Western Hemisphere which came with the victory. Toward the end of his term at the Point MacArthur married Louise Cromwell Brooks, a rich divorcee. The marriage was a failure, and there was a Reno divorce in 1929.

In 1922 MacArthur was appointed to command the Manila district in the Philippines after he had made certain that the number of cadets at the Point was increased to nearly double its former size. MacArthur was happy to be back in the Philippines after so many years, and he was delighted to see that so much had been accomplished in his absence. Local autonomous government, under the guidance of Manuel Quezon, was moving forward, and roads, hospitals, schools, docks and buildings of all sorts had appeared. General Leonard Wood, former hero of the Spanish-American War and unsuccessful Presidential candidate in 1920, had been appointed Governor General, but Wood was a stone in the path of the Philippine desire to achieve national independence as soon as possible. MacArthur, on the other hand, was very friendly indeed with the Filipinos, and his rather out-

spoken opposition to those who stood in the way of the Philippine desire to achieve independence won resentment for his presence. All the same, MacArthur was given the job of drawing up a plan for the defense of the Bataan Peninsula, near Manila, and he covered every foot of the rugged terrain there.

In 1925 he was transferred to Baltimore and was detailed to be a member of the court which was to try MacArthur's old friend, Billy Mitchell, who had criticized the American government's failure to develop her air power after the United States had made a start on forming the nucleus of an air force during World War I. MacArthur considered his presence on the court to have been one of the most distasteful experiences of his life, and the court martial sentenced Billy Mitchell to suspension from duty for two and a half years, after which he resigned. MacArthur was subsequently accused of having let his friend down, but MacArthur explained that he had always believed (as future events were to prove) that a senior officer should not be

Below: MacArthur with Governor of the Philippines Henry L Stimson in 1928. Stimson later served in the cabinet of three Presidents, Hoover, Roosevelt and Truman.

Above: MacArthur (right) awaits the arrival of a transport ship in Manila in June 1929.

silenced for disagreeing with his superiors in rank and with accepted doctrine. He knew that Mitchell's paramount interest was in the future security of his country, but courts martial of the type Mitchell was subjected to only require a two-thirds vote of its members to convict. MacArthur probably did not vote for conviction, and he later said that Mitchell 'was wrong in the violence of his language . . . [but] that he was right in his thesis is equally true and incontrovertible.'

In 1927 MacArthur was released from his army appointment to serve as President of the American Olympic Committee, and the American team made an excellent performance at the Games held in 1928 in Amsterdam. After the Games MacArthur resumed his army appointment and was sent once more to the Philippines as commander of the Philippine Department, as the American

army command there was called. He resumed his association with Quezon, with whom he became extremely friendly, as well as with Henry L Stimson, former Secretary of War, now Governor General, who was more in sympathy with both MacArthur's and the Filipinos' views on the achievement of independence for the archipelago. He discussed with both Quezon and Stimson the problem of Japan, which had expressed concern about the situation in China, especially after Chiang Kaishek had unified the country after his successful march to the north. Japan had made a claim to having special interests in North China and for years had maintained a certain control over Manchuria through her ownership of the South Manchurian Railway and the maintenance of her troops in the area to protect the railroads. Furthermore Japanese immigration to the Philippine island of Mindanao was on the increase, much to the consternation of Quezon and MacArthur. Although the resources at hand were pitifully inadequate, Mac-

Arthur did what he could to improve the forces defending the islands, but it became increasingly apparent that unless the islands' defenses were vastly improved, the Philippines could one day be caught in a struggle for power in the Western Pacific that would inevitably involve the United States. MacArthur's warnings, in the international atmosphere which produced the Kellogg-Briand Pact, which abolished war as an instrument of national policy for virtually all the nations of the world who signed it – a treaty dubbed by cynical observers at the time as 'an international kiss' – went unheeded.

In July 1929 MacArthur was informed that President Hoover wanted to appoint him Chief of Engineers. MacArthur declined on the grounds that he lacked the engineering expertise that the job demanded and therefore would not have the confidence of the engineering profession. It was one of the wisest decisions MacArthur ever made, as Hoover subsequently offered him the post of Chief of Staff with the

rank of full general to succeed General Summerall whose four-year term was to expire in November 1930. MacArthur later recalled that he shrank from the responsibility, 'and wished from the bottom of my heart to stay with troops in a field command. But my mother, who made her home in Washington, sensed what was in my mind and cabled me to accept. She said my father would be ashamed if I showed timidity. That settled it.'

MacArthur came to the post just as the depression was making itself felt throughout the country and the world, and at a time when the US Army was at its lowest point since before the Spanish-American War. It needed the dynamism of a younger, more vigorous man, which MacArthur was. He was, in fact, the youngest Chief of Staff since that office was established 27 years before; and his career at West Point and in the war amply prepared him for that high office. His chief problem, however, was maintaining enough money year after year to sustain at least the basis of a

Above: MacArthur is sworn in as Chief of Staff, US Army on 12 November 1930 by Edward Kreger, Judge Advocate General of the Army and Secretary of War Patrick Hurley.

Left: MacArthur, in full general's uniform, gives orders to a brigadier general during the operations undertaken against the Bonus Marchers.

Below: MacArthur with President Hoover on the dais in 1932 as a military parade passes by on Washington's birthday which some 15 million unemployed celebrated that year.

modern army as well as reequiping an army which had little more than what it possessed in 1918.

The American army was weak, small and lumbered with obsolete equipment. In 1930, when he took command, the army only had 125,000 men and some 12,000 officers. When he left the post five years later the figures were about the

same. All this took place at a time when the annual national expenditure for the army decreased each year except for the last, 1935, when it increased fractionally. However, MacArthur managed to increase the cadet corps at West Point almost to the level that he had initially proposed for it when he was Superintendent – from 1374 to 1960 men. For the sake of comparison it is useful to point out that Britain's standing army was around 230,000 at this time and the USSR's, 624,000. Germany, prior to Hitler's takeover, had an army limited by the Treaty of Versailles to a number in excess of what the United States maintained in the early 1930s. Small wonder, then, that MacArthur felt that for a population almost three times that of Britain and well over twice that of Germany (at that time) the United States was dangerously under-strength and, furthermore, under-equipped to fight modern war. Nevertheless, it was difficult to focus public attention on subjects other than those which alleviated unemployment and raised the standard of living during the Depression.

It was very likely at this time, if at no time before this, that MacArthur began to realize fully the importance of public opinion in maintaining support of the armed forces. The master of the battlefield, as he feared before he took the office of Chief of Staff, would find himself in entirely different waters as a general *cum* politician. Every successful

Above: MacArthur shares emergency rations with the men during the operations against the Bonus Marchers. Several of their camps were burned during that night.

general on as high a level as MacArthur attained has, in the end, to cope with civil officials unless, of course, the state is controlled directly by the military. Such a circumstance exists in both democratic as well as authoritarian countries. In a democracy such as the United States, however, it is imperative that the generals of the army, and especially the Chief of Staff, have close working relationships with their civilian masters. No matter what lack of expertise the soldier may think resides with the leaders of government at any given point in history, if a democracy of any sort is to be maintained, the generals must accept the fact that whether they like it or not, they are not the supreme arbiters of the state. Therefore, to achieve what they desire, they must turn to their elected masters for support. To turn to the public over the heads of their elected representatives is to court disaster. It must be said, in all fairness, that thoughts of a military coup or of appealing over the head of state to the people probably did not occur to MacArthur at this time, as they were to do later, but it is clear that getting along with and cajoling the President and the

Secretary of the Army was necessary to improve the deplorable state the army was in when MacArthur became its Chief of Staff.

MacArthur's main tasks, realizing that neither the Republican government of Herbert Hoover, nor the Democratic government of Franklin D Roosevelt, which replaced it in 1933, would countenance vast increases in federal spending on the armed services during MacArthur's term of office, were to concentrate on improving the equipment of the army and reorganizing it. He experimented with the development of modern tanks, which he felt vital to the defense of the United States, and he wanted to ensure that if another war broke out, the United States would manufacture the most modern military machinery rather than obsolete types. MacArthur also made certain that the Congress did not cut federal appropriations to the army by reducing its officer corps by an additional 2000 men. The vote in the Congress was close – one vote in the House of Representatives – but the army's officer corps was not reduced. It was a shallow victory but MacArthur won. He also made sure that, with what resources he had at hand, he would try to develop the nucleus of a modern air force to be attached to the army as a whole and placed directly under the Chief of

Staff rather than attached to any specific unit. He also reorganized the army so that four armies would be formed which would embrace the whole of the United States.

As Chief of Staff MacArthur made two trips to Europe, the first in 1931. In France he watched, at the invitation of the French government, the annual maneuvers which included the replacement of mounted horse cavalry with fast, heavily armored tanks, which impressed him and made him even more certain that the United States should do the same. On his second trip to France in 1932 he was again impressed by the degree of mechanization that the French had put into their armed forces, even during the economic slump which affected her as much as it did the United States. Germany was closer to France than it was to the United States. President Hindenburg of Germany openly stated that the most vulnerable targets in the next war would be the great industrial centers with their massive populations. King Alexander showed MacArthur his oxcarts which were meant to supply his Serbian divisions. Admiral Horthy of Hungary spoke of impending disaster internationally, as did Jozef Pilsudski of Poland, while he noticed that Czechoslovakia was building munitions plants feverishly. It took no military or political expert to recognize the dangers inherent in the coming of Adolf Hitler to power in 1933 and what this could mean for the future of Europe and the United States, whose histories have been so intertwined since the founding of the American Republic. Yet Hitler was considered to be a crank by most Americans – at least at first. Japan's invasion of Manchuria in 1931 and its penetration of Inner Mongolia in 1933 were viewed as unfortunate, perhaps, but certainly not as important as licking the Depression. Despite MacArthur's warnings little could be done within the political and social framework of the times.

The times were difficult indeed. With over a quarter of the working population unemployed by 1932, even MacArthur was forced to turn his attentions to dealing with the Depression by military means; veterans of the American Expeditionary Force, who had been promised a bonus soon after the end of the war, and who were subsequently compensated for their services in the form of insurance policies, were anxious to collect the face value of their policies as well as their long-promised bonus straightaway, without waiting for them to mature. These men were out of work, some of them homeless, many of them hungry. Thousands of them marched to Washington in the summer of 1932 to demand their bonus payments, and they set up their makeshift camps on the Anacostia Flats near the Capitol. Others occupied partly demolished buildings along Pennsylvania Avenue.

MacArthur had never been a political radical. On the contrary he looked upon the Bonus Marchers as unfortunates, to be sure, but probably infiltrated by Communists. However, initially MacArthur ordered tents and camping equipment to be sent to the Flats for the marchers and ordered out a number of rolling kitchens to help feed the multitude. This last step raised a controversy within the Congress. One Representative mentioned that if the government provided the marchers with three meals a day, hundreds of thousands of hungry Americans might make their way to Washington to join the bonus army. In this enlightened mood, the kitchens were withdrawn. In the punishing heat of a Washington summer, combined with the inaction of President Hoover,

the bonus boys became increasingly disgruntled. Hoover offered to pay the marchers' bus fare home if they would only leave. Governor Franklin D Roosevelt of New York informed all New Yorkers within the ranks of the bonus army that they would be given train fares home by the state if they would only leave. The Bonus Marchers would not leave.

On 28 July the police began to evict the squatters living between the Capitol and the business district. There was a clash and a policeman shot and killed one marcher. MacArthur maintained later that there were few *bona fide*

Below: MacArthur headed the troops which dispersed the Bonus marchers in the summer of 1932 in Washington. Aided by Eisenhower and Patton the army burned the veterans' shantytowns (Hoovervilles).

veterans in the group and that they were under the influence of Communist agitators. This presumption was most unlikely. There were probably a few Communists in the crowd, but most of the marchers were protesting a genuine grievance, and the American public was anxious to see how the veterans of World War I were going to be treated. MacArthur received an order from the Secretary of War, Patrick J Hurley, that the President had informed him that the civil government of the District of Columbia was unable to maintain law and order, and that MacArthur was to direct United States troops to the 'scene of disorder,' to surround the area and to clear it without delay. He was also admonished to 'use all humanity consistent with the due execution of the order.' About 600

infantry and cavalry as well as a platoon of tanks were ready. Accompanied by two of his staff officers, Major Dwight D Eisenhower and Major George S Patton, MacArthur proceeded on horseback to the area where the squatters resisted. By the evening of 28 July the Bonus Army was driven back across the Anacostia River to their camp. Not a shot was fired and no one was seriously hurt. At 2100 hours the troops were ordered to clear the Anacostia Flats. By the next morning most marchers had gone, and tear gas was used to repel the marchers who stayed to throw rocks at the soldiers. Those who still remained in parts of the city were removed the rest of the following day. MacArthur apparently had won another victory, but a hollow one.

MacArthur insisted that it was a Communist plot and, in fact, a few Communists were arrested. The Communist Party of the United States,

Below: MacArthur and Roosevelt's Secretary of War George Dern prepare to enter a car to visit maneuvers at Fort Monmouth, New Jersey in 1934.

apparently in a spirit of bravado, claimed responsibility for the bonus march; of course they would. Most of the American people sympathized with the marchers. In fact, most of the marchers were ordinary Americans who had felt that their government had given them a raw deal and they wanted to protest about it and to get the money they felt they deserved. MacArthur took a beating from the national press for his involvement in the affair. He even sued Drew Pearson and Robert S Allen, well-known left-of-center newspaper columnists, for damages amounting to $1,750,000 for their criticisms of him, depicting MacArthur as a pompous man-on-horseback who had turned on his former comrades-in-arms. He soon realized it was a mistake and dropped the case. Actually, there was nothing offensive in what MacArthur did. He merely followed orders, as the saying goes. No one was killed, few were seriously hurt, but the sight of the burning camps and the sight of the smoke from these camps slowly drifting over and blackening the Capitol of the United States infuriated millions of

Americans. The Bonus Marchers and their fate became a symbol of the inability of the Republican government to cope with the problems of the Depression. MacArthur became, in the eyes of many, a symbol of repression and right-wing fanaticism which he was unable to shake off throughout his career. MacArthur may have technically done no wrong in this incident, but he was politically naive, and was stung deeply by the criticism he had to endure. MacArthur was soon to learn that it did not pay for a general to be politically naive.

Franklin D Roosevelt succeeded Hoover on 4 March 1933, at a time when the country had hit rock bottom. The new President was a very different sort of man from Hoover, and had promised a 'New Deal' to the American people who were crying out for leadership. His Hundred Days of Reform brought a new spirit of optimism to the United States, which slowly began to move forward again under his leadership. One of the sweeping reforms made in these early days was to provide money to employ some 300,000 in reforestation work throughout the country. The army

Above: MacArthur addressing military training students at the close of a camp at Fort Howard, Maryland. MacArthur continued to exhort the government for military and defense spending.

was to organize these men into units, equip them and transport them to their places of employment, where the civil authorities would establish their camps and supervise their efforts. Civilian officials were unable to cope, however, and the army took over the entire operation with great efficiency. The CCC camps, as they were known (Civilian Conservation Corps), became one of the most popular early successes of the Roosevelt administration.

Roosevelt's relations with MacArthur, which were to become stormier as time went on – because of the differing political philosophies of the two men as much as the fact that both were strong personalities who inevitably rubbed against each other the wrong way – began on a shaky footing when Roosevelt's new Secretary of War, George H Dern, was faced with a cut in army appropriations of around $30,000,000. MacArthur, aided by Dern, vigorously

opposed these measures, which Mac-Arthur felt would force 3–4000 officers into retirement, discharge 12–15,000 men from the forces, eliminate field and armory drill training of the National Guard, and almost completely dismantle the technical services of the army. MacArthur arranged with Dern to see FDR. MacArthur pointed out that the world situation was too dangerous to allow a further weakening of American defenses while Germany, Italy and Japan were busy rearming. Roosevelt poured sarcasm over MacArthur's remarks, and then MacArthur's temper got the better of him. He said words to the effect that if America lost the next war he wanted the American soldier dying in the mud to spit out the name 'Roosevelt' before he died, not 'Mac-Arthur.' Roosevelt, quite naturally, objected vehemently to MacArthur's intemperate and melodramatic tone and shouted at him, 'You must not talk that way to the President.' MacArthur apologized and offered to resign as Chief of Staff. As he walked out of the door Roosevelt coolly remarked, 'Don't be foolish, Douglas; you and the budget

must get together on this.' Dern came to him afterward as they were walking out and gleefully told him, 'you've saved the army.' MacArthur recalled in his memoirs: 'but I just vomited on the steps of the White House.'

After that stormy incident MacArthur reported that from then on Roosevelt was on the army's side. MacArthur's resignation was not accepted and as a matter of fact, Roosevelt extended his term as Chief of Staff for one year in 1934, an unusual event at that time. Army appropriations were cut, but Mac-Arthur managed with what he had by adopting a policy of limiting the army to development of pilot models of new equipment rather than committing itself to large-scale manufacture of weapons that in the course of a short period of time would become obsolete. Such a policy had a great appeal in a country like the United States which was not likely to be invaded by land, and at a time when money was short. He realized that military plans and preparation take a number of years, but warned that a sufficient nucleus of an armed force must be maintained so that when danger

Above: Secretary of War Dern pins the Distinguished Service Medal on MacArthur in 1935 on the occasion of his retirement from the US Army.

threatened or when better economic prospects were in sight it could swiftly be built up again. His organizational reforms were cited upon his retirement as Chief of Staff in 1935, when he was awarded an Oak Leaf Cluster to his Distinguished Service Medal, for his work in creating an Army Air Corps.

When he retired there was no place for MacArthur to go. It is more than likely that Roosevelt was happy to be rid of him so that a more like-minded individual could take his place. It was fortunate for both MacArthur and Roosevelt that Manuel Quezon, MacArthur's old friend from the Philippines, which had by now become a Commonwealth of the United States had called on MacArthur in 1934 while he was still Chief of Staff. Commonwealth status in the American sense means a certain nominal independence, but with foreign affairs and major problems of defense as well as a few other reserve powers retained by the government in Washington. The Philippines had been told that this status would last for 10 years, after which they could become independent. Quezon had initially called on MacArthur to discuss problems of Philippine national defense after the country had achieved independence. He asked if the islands were defensible. MacArthur replied that if sufficient money, men and

munitions were made available as well as enough time to train the troops, provide the munitions and raise the money, any place was defensible. Quezon asked him if, upon his retirement as Chief of Staff, he would undertake the job and MacArthur replied that he would. But he also warned that it would take at least 10 years with considerable help from the United States for the defense of the Philippines to be accomplished.

Soon after this meeting Roosevelt asked MacArthur to see him and told him that with the inauguration of the Commonwealth, the governor general-ship would lapse and be replaced by a high commissioner. The job could be his. This proposal would involve Mac-Arthur's retirement from the army. MacArthur told the President that he had started as a soldier and wanted to end as one. A compromise was reached whereby MacArthur would do the job he was requested to do as a servant of the Philippine government, whose army would be developed independently of but in cooperation with the American garrison: the Philippine Department of the United States Army, which Mac-Arthur once headed. Its leader at that time, Major General Lucius R Holbrook, was instructed to give all assistance possible to MacArthur.

At the age of 55 MacArthur was to embark upon a new career, but far enough away from Washington so that he could have no real political influence where it mattered. It could be said that Roosevelt wanted to maneuver Mac-Arthur into this backwater, but in actual fact there was no place for Mac-Arthur to go but the Philippines. He had an emotional and traditional attachment to the islands, and considered them his second home. It was a job which was likely to keep him busy until he was 66, at which point, barring any unforeseen circumstances, he could retire to write his memoirs. MacArthur, however, did not consider the Philippines a backwater as Roosevelt might have done. He realiz-ed full well that a conflict in the Far East with Japan was only a matter of time, and that, out of a sense of loyalty to the island Commonwealth, he ought to do

Right: General MacArthur receiving escort honors from the 31st Infantry upon his arrival in Manila in October 1935. Major Eisenhower is left of MacArthur.

what he could to improve its defenses which he felt were imperative to the defense of the United States itself. Before he left Washington, however, he reestablished the Order of the Purple Heart, given to men wounded in action, a decoration which had not been used in over a century, and one which antedates almost all of the famous military medals in the world. It was one which was to be given many times before MacArthur left the Philippines again.

Just before he left for his new post MacArthur was given another medal of his own: his second Distinguished Service Medal. He sailed for the Philippines in the fall of 1935 on the *President Hoover* from San Francisco; his fifth tour in the Far East; and the most important mission in his life.

MacArthur's staff as Military Adviser of the Philippine Commonwealth consisted of four officers, among them Major D Eisenhower and James B Ord. Eisenhower greatly impressed MacArthur when he was on MacArthur's staff in Washington, and he and Ord helped draw up a plan for a Philippine National Defense Act, which intended to provide a militia of about 200,000 men organized into small divisions of about 7500 each, a small air corps, and marines equipped with torpedo boats. With the reserve the total within 10 years would come to about 400,000.

However, the plan ran into difficulties almost from the beginning. There was a movement afoot in the islands to reject the idea of national independence and to depend entirely upon the United States for defense, which Quezon and MacArthur crushed. There was a great deal of public doubt and apathy surrounding the project, and Quezon vigorously tried to combat this by telling his people that the only hope for peace in the Western Pacific was to rearm. Quezon had agreed with MacArthur that the Philippine government would provide $7,500,000–10,000,000 per annum to fulfil their military requirements. Quezon was unable to meet these requirements. The budget dropped to only $6,000,000 and heavy opposition grew against the rearmament program. The rearmament proposals themselves had certain serious flaws. For one thing, there was no provision made for a battle fleet to protect the islands. MacArthur explained that since his mission was of a

Above: An antiquated artillery piece in an open-topped emplacement on Corregidor. MacArthur had warned the US that such defenses were inadequate and he was proved right.

defensive character, only the interior waterways of the islands needed protection, which could be accomplished by torpedo boats, which could 'deny the enemy an opportunity to bring its forces close enough to Philippine shores to debark his troops and supplies.'

The whole idea was mistaken from the start. To imagine that a few torpedo boats and a hundred bombers could prevent invasion of the dozens of islands of the Philippines by Japan was either naive or irresponsible. It is true to say that the Philippine government was unprepared to pay for the construction or purchase of a large defensive navy, but the fact that the United States was unprepared to defend the islands with its own under-equipped navy was hidden from the Philippine government and people. One could argue the point that since neither the American nor the Philippine government, because of the economic crisis and public apathy, could do much about making a realistic defense of the Philippines, the brave words emanating from time to time from MacArthur and Quezon would keep morale high. One could counter that argument by stating that the disillusionment would be all the greater if the shaky defense program was ever put to the test, and that it helped create further apathy by lulling the population into

thinking that everything was really all right. The best that can be said for MacArthur's policy was that he contributed something to the defense of the islands. Events were to prove that what was done was far from adequate, and that the exposure of the shores of the island Commonwealth to the huge Japanese Navy was downright scandalous. In MacArthur's defense one could say that whatever measures were taken they would have been inadequate anyway, but a more realistic attempt should certainly have been made.

For example, the training of groups of recruits and then sending them home to train new groups was no way to form an effective army. A better plan might have been to train at least skeleton regiments and divisions from the start so that effective training could proceed at all levels. Even in this plan MacArthur lacked vision. He proposed an initial call-up of only 3000, whereas Quezon insisted on the full quota of 20,000 in 1937. The result was that instructors were pretty thin on the ground, and the idea of saving money in the first years in order to be able to spend it later on did not work. The training of strong cadres prepared to fight would have taken large numbers of American officers and NCOs, which were not forthcoming from Washington. Intensive training of Filipino officers to fill the gap did not take place. MacArthur felt that half-trained cadres could tie the Japanese down to fighting protracted guerrilla warfare which could slow down their war effort if they launched a full-scale invasion of Southeast Asia and the Western Pacific. If the whole army had been indoctrinated with guerrilla tactics from the start the plan might have been effective, but since they were not, the Philippine army could only prove a nuisance to a highly effective, well-equipped Japanese army invading by sea.

The fault cannot be laid entirely at the feet of MacArthur. He noted that a certain coolness grew between Quezon and Roosevelt which made requests to Washington for aid all the more difficult. Roosevelt, seeing the problem, offered MacArthur a new command which was to consist of the entire Pacific, including Hawaii and the American west coast. MacArthur refused, since he had promised Quezon that he would remain as

Below: MacArthur and Manuel Quezon, President of the Philippines, at the outbreak of war in the Pacific in late 1941.

adviser throughout Quezon's six-year term as President of the Commonwealth, which would end in 1943. Roosevelt's anger with MacArthur apparently was growing over the years. Their political philosophies were poles apart: their manner, though equally grandiose in style, had an important difference. Roosevelt got what he wanted through cunning and occasional guile. MacArthur's strong suit was hauteur and remoteness. The charm of his early years had gone. His mother, who had come with him to Manila, had died, and since his brother and father were gone, MacArthur was alone. He spent his spare time going to the movies almost every night and his remote disposition was intensified. His marriage to Jean Marie Faircloth in 1937 did much to alleviate this loneliness. The following year his son, Arthur, was born, and this renewal of family life did a lot for MacArthur, as he admitted himself. The distance between him and his President was not narrowed by his new family responsibilities; the damage

had been done and the rift was to widen.

In 1937 MacArthur made another trip, this time with Quezon to Japan, as well as Mexico and the United States, where MacArthur married his second wife. He was impressed and worried by Japan's obvious military buildup and the invasion of China proper was soon to begin. He realized at this point that in order to carry on their policy of expansion, the Japanese needed the oil and rubber of the Dutch East Indies as well as Malaya's tin and nickel, not to mention the great rice basin of Burma and Thailand. The Philippines stood in the way of that expansion, and although there was little that the islands had which the Japanese needed for their war effort, MacArthur believed that it was only a matter of time before the Japanese would try to seize the islands as part of a southward expansion policy. This need not necessarily have been the case; the Japanese might have bypassed the Philippines, but it stood to reason that if Japan planned to move southward one day,

Above: B-18 bombers raid Japanese positions on Luzon on 10 December 1941. Only 125 of some 300 US aircraft were fit for combat then.

the Philippines would block the path. MacArthur was all the more determined to continue the military buildup of the islands. When he arrived in Washington he had to make a decision about taking up Roosevelt's offer to return to take command of the defense of Hawaii and the west coast. MacArthur, feeling that he was blocking the promotion of subordinates, took the step of retiring from the army and being appointed Field Marshal of the Philippines, a rank which did not and still does not exist in the American army, and a title which MacArthur dearly loved.

If MacArthur, the Philippine government and the American government did little to substantially improve the islands' defenses, at least MacArthur was able to improve morale. Acting on the assumption that grandeur impressed Asians, MacArthur succeeded in impressing the Filipinos with his sense of authority, if not infallibility. The pomp and ceremony of his unique office, the freedom to give full rein to his sense of the melodramatic, the gold braid and the new cap which he helped design himself, all served to create a public personality which slowly eradicated what was left of the genuine military hero of World War I. MacArthur could get away with the sort of thing in Manila which would have raised eyebrows and sniggers in Washington. More important, the restraints naturally imposed upon him by his own government, by other high ranking members of the military élite and by the President were removed

in his new status in the Philippines. His chief of staff, General Richard K Sutherland, tended to ape the mannerisms of his superior. He was hard to handle, arrogant, autocratic and short-tempered, the wrong sort of person for the job. MacArthur did little or nothing to curb these tendencies in his chief of staff, and the atmosphere around MacArthur became more that of a court than a military headquarters.

This absorption of MacArthur's private personality by his public, or rather, the merger of the two, struck many of his other subordinates as excessive. Major Eisenhower was one of them, and was recorded to have later remarked, when asked by a woman whether he had met MacArthur, 'Not only have I met him, madam, but I studied dramatics under him for five years in Washington and four in the Philippines.' He left MacArthur for another post during MacArthur's reign in Manila. Others like General Lewis H Brereton, were favorably impressed. He described MacArthur as 'one of the most beautiful talkers I have ever heard, and while his manner might be considered a bit on the theatrical side, it is just a part of his personality.' MacArthur had found a new role: one of acting the part of an absolute monarch; and one which he was to resume in Japan after the war.

The heady atmosphere of those Manila days before World War II and the lack of criticism of MacArthur which accompanied them was upset by the outbreak of war in Europe and the expansion of Japan's military involvement in China. By 1939 Japan had seized virtually the whole east coast of China facing the Philippines, and by mid-1940, after the fall of France and the Low Countries,

Japan intensified her political and economic pressure on the isolated Dutch East Indies and invaded Tonking, later to become part of northern Vietnam, and then part of French Indo-China. The United States adopted a position of thinly disguised neutrality toward these actions, and worked behind the scenes to bolster the resolve of the French and Dutch colonial governments in Southeast Asia, achieving considerable success with respect to the latter, if not the former. A series of economic sanctions was imposed on Japan by the United States, which only encouraged Japan's resolve to expand into the rest of Southeast Asia, rather than acting as a deterrent, as the Americans hoped.

It would have been sensible at this time for the Philippine government, acting on MacArthur's advice, to have called its armed forces together, or carried out a trial mobilization in order to test their organization. The new commander of the Philippine Department, Major General George Grunert, was appointed in June 1940 and he immediately asked for more men and equipment. Initially there was no response from Washington. Grunert pressed the point, arguing that the Philippine government no longer believed that the United States was prepared to defend the islands, and he recommended that a strong air and submarine force be established while US Army units built up and trained the Philippine army. Quezon supported this request, but again no action was taken.

President Roosevelt had trouble enough in gaining the support necessary to introduce conscription, which finally passed the Congress in the autumn of 1940 and which permitted the United States to establish an army of almost a million and a half as well as the mobilization of the National Guard.

Roosevelt wanted to help, but there was little he could do other than the actions which he did take. The trouble was, however, that Roosevelt's main concern was with Europe, not Asia. He believed that the takeover of Western Europe by Hitler posed a greater danger to American security than the Japanese takeover of northern Indo-China. There are few people today who would doubt Roosevelt's judgment, but there were many at that time who did: they resented the fact that when Lend-Lease was finally enacted, most of the aid went to Britain, and very little to the Pacific area; that when the destroyer-base deal was concluded, the naval assistance went to secure Britain in the North Atlantic and in the North Sea, rather than to Singapore or Hong Kong. Isolationists tended to thinly disguise a definable Anglophobia and, sometimes, a certain recognition of the advantages a Nazi-controlled European continent might offer. These same groups and individuals, on the other hand, tended to stress the importance of the Pacific as a primary area of American interest, rather than a decadent and ungrateful Europe. MacArthur was more in this camp than in the camp of Roosevelt and the Europefirsters, and this was another cause of the rift between Roosevelt and MacArthur that was to increasingly damage the US position in the Far East.

In all fairness, however, it must be mentioned that America was just be-

Below: Henry J Kaiser presents President Roosevelt with a model escort carrier. The industrial power of the US was rightly feared by moderate Japanese.

ginning its military buildup in 1940, that priorities had to be given for the limited resources America had at its disposal at that time. Roosevelt, after all, chose the right priority, however desirable it might have been to be able to train the American army at home, develop the necessary material of war, supply Britain and later, Russia, with whatever could be spared, rearm and reequip an out-of-date navy and a virtually non-existent air corps and, at the same time, supply the Philippines with arms, men, training and a fleet. The Philippines were toward the bottom of America's list of priorities. The Dutch East Indies, with the oil and rubber and tin, which the United States so desperately needed and which Japan coveted, could be supplied with little or nothing from America's growing but still small storehouse of weapons and ships. The American government urged the Netherlands Indies government to resist Japanese demands for more goods, but could do little more than that. The Dutch East Indies was far more important, strategically and in terms of natural resources, to the United

States and its defense than its own Commonwealth was. Small wonder that MacArthur and Grunert were disappointed in Roosevelt's lack of response.

Yet further requests were forthcoming from Manila. In November 1940 General George C Marshall in Washington was told by Grunert that the Philippine army possessed 12 divisions comprising 120,000 trained men, but made it clear that the bulk of these were in reserve and not on active duty. About half of the officers, however, had no training and no unit larger than a battalion had ever been assembled for field training; it was a paper army. Grunert proposed that, in the event of an attack, Filipinos should be used in companies and battalions with an American officer commanding each company. He also recommended that Filipino units be mobilized immediately and asked for 500 officers. In response to this request 75 were sent and the proposal to mobilize the army was rejected due to lack of funds. By the first of the year, however, Washington relented a little. It was decided to send 60 field artillery weapons and 20 old antiaircraft guns as reinforcements.

Above: The 4th Marines in retreat on the Bataan Peninsula. The US and Philippine forces had to retreat to this redoubt when the Japanese overran Luzon in 1941–42.

Despite these pitiful responses Mac-Arthur held an optimistic view. He stated that the Philippines would be able to defend themselves if given enough time; the target date was 1946. He suggested that it would cost an enemy at least a half a million casualties and 'upwards of five billion dollars' to succeed in invading the islands. In a letter to Marshall in February 1941 he described his mission as one of preparing the Philippines to be able to resist an enemy attack by 1946, and that the planned army of a quarter of a million men would be ready by the end of 1941. This, plus his small air force and 30–50 motor torpedo boats, he reckoned, could provide 'an adequate defense at the beach against a landing operation by an expeditionary force of 100,000 which is estimated to be the maximum initial effort of the most powerful potential enemy.'

MacArthur envisaged defending not only Manila Bay and Luzon but the Visayas as well (the central islands of the Philippines) by blocking the straits leading to its inland seas. Therefore, he reported that he would need seven 12-inch guns, 25 155-mm guns and 32 mobile searchlights. He was told that the heavy guns would not be available until 1943 and the medium guns and searchlights not until 1942. Even these feeble efforts, which appear optimistic to say the least to repel a heavily armed and prepared Japanese invader, were thwarted by Washington. When asked to comment, Grunert repeated the fact that the Philippine army 'had practically no field training nor target practice.' The Philippine defense force had, at this time, 42 aircraft and two torpedo boats.

In April 1941 staff talks were held between British, American and Netherlands Indies officers to plan the defense of Southeast Asia against what they presumed to be an inevitable Japanese attack. The assumption again was made, with the unenthusiastic and begrudged approval of her Allies, that the United States, which potentially had the most to offer the area in the way of specific arms, planes and ships, would concentrate its war effort (once America was in the war: this too was presumed) on victory in Europe rather than Asia. A defensive posture, a holding operation, was the most that could be hoped for in the Western Pacific.

These Singapore talks suggested that the defenses of Luzon be strengthened and that a bomber force be created there so that a bombing offensive could later be launched against the home islands of Japan. General Grunert remarked afterward that 'our present mission and restrictions as to means are not in accord' with this report. By this time the decision had been reached to move some of the American Pacific fleet to the Atlantic so that the ratio between the Atlantic and Pacific fleets would be 60:40. Furthermore, Secretary of War, former Governor General of the Philippines, Henry L Stimson, approved. On 26 July 1941 MacArthur was given charge of US Army Forces in the Far East.

It is interesting to note that just before this appointment was made the Japanese moved into southern Indo-China and that weeks before that, the Japanese negotiations with the Dutch in Batavia, capital of the Dutch East Indies, had broken down; the Dutch had refused to fulfil the lavish requests made by Japan for strategic raw materials, although they had come some of the way toward a settlement. On 26 July, the day of Mac-Arthur's appointment, the United States, followed almost immediately by Britain and Holland, froze Japanese assets in their respective areas. The Allies knew that this act, which would not allow Japan supplies she needed to continue the war in China, much less allow her to persevere in actions anywhere else, was tantamount to a declaration of war. It was now only a matter of counting the days until she either backed down, which seemed highly unlikely, or went to war. MacArthur was given the rank of major general, but the next day was promoted to lieutenant general; five months later he regained the rank of general.

As commander of United States Army Forces in the Far East (USAFFE) MacArthur formed a new staff, comprising many members of his old team, which remained largely intact throughout the course of the war. Sutherland stayed on as his chief of staff and his senior intelligence officer was Lieutenant Colonel Charles A Willoughby, who was to lead

Below: Filipino scouts after a successful raid on a Japanese position in Luzon. The scouts carried on bravely in a hopeless cause.

his intelligence team from then on and who was, incidentally, a naturalized American of German origin. MacArthur's initial plan was to defend Manila Bay above all until reinforcements could arrive; this was similar to Britain's position in Singapore.

There were those who criticized this plan, critics who felt that defending the Philippines was a waste of energy and manpower, and that the United States would do better by acquiescing in the temporary loss of the Commonwealth. Australians felt that Singapore had insufficient defenses and that it was vulnerable on the landward side. MacArthur however worked on the presumption that although he still needed five more years for the Philippines to be

impregnable, he could put up a decent defense of the islands. Realizing that his weakest element was the air, he sought to establish a supply link of airfields stretching from lower Mindanao to upper Luzon which would be connected with airfields in Australia, the Dutch East Indies and Malaya. By October nine new B-17 bombers had arrived at Clark Field outside Manila as well as 50 pursuit planes. By December, however, American operational air forces totalled only 35 bombers and 72 pursuit planes, less than half of what MacArthur felt was necessary. Even this hoped-for total was far short of what was required. On the seas, over which MacArthur had no direct authority, the situation was pitifully weak, even worse than the lack

Above: Chairman of the Joint Chiefs of Staff General George C Marshall confers with Secretary of War Henry L Stimson in January 1942.

of air strength. The entire fleet was composed of three cruisers, 13 destroyers 18 submarines and six PT boats.

MacArthur's assessment still included a fairly optimistic appraisal of the coming crisis. He expected that the Japanese would land with a force of about 100,000 men, and that they would make a surprise attack on the islands somewhere around December 1941 or January 1942. American efforts would concentrate on preventing them from landing, but if this failed the defending army would be withdrawn to the Bataan Peninsula, the key to the control of Manila Bay and the last redoubt of the American forces. The plan presumed that Japanese forces could be held long enough for reinforcements to reach Bataan, which was supposed to be able to hold off the Japanese for 180 days, after which the American forces, if not reinforced, would be forced to capitulate. This plan, however, was soon abandoned and replaced with a new one, which also rejected another scheme, Rainbow 5, which implicitly accepted the loss of the Philippines and which recognized Germany as the principal opponent of the

United States. Major General Lewis Brereton arrived with the plan on 3 November when he came to Manila to take command of MacArthur's air force. It was a letter from Marshall authorizing MacArthur to defend the whole archipelago. MacArthur welcomed this news, without recognizing the impossibility of putting the new plan into effect. MacArthur tended to underestimate the Japanese and seized upon any information he heard which tended to presume Japan's weakness or war-weariness from her struggle in China.

What caused the change of heart in Washington? One reason was undoubtedly MacArthur's continued optimism, as expressed in his reports to Washington. If he, with all his experience and knowledge of the situation on the spot, felt that the islands could be defended, Washington was not going to stand in his way. The other reason could have been the great potential shown by British Flying Fortresses operating against Germany from the UK. But, as MacArthur reported himself, there were only 35 bombers in the Philippines by December. In October Secretary of War Stimson told the Secretary of State, Cordell Hull, that time was needed to prepare the islands; three months. At this point there were less than two months to go. By December there were only 61 of the

B-17 heavy bombers at American bases outside the United States and not many more existed in the States. There were less than 24 B-17s in Britain at this time. Thus, based largely on MacArthur's optimism, a group of obsolete aircraft supported by a few modern ones, a navy which hardly existed at all and an army which was ill-prepared and which consisted of not more than about 22,000 men under arms was preparing to take on the strength of Imperial Japan. Even by comparison with the British force in Malaya at this time, the American force in the Philippines was weak.

MacArthur decided to mobilize his reserves, but since there were not enough quarters to accommodate the 75,000 men of the 10 reserve divisions, he then decided to call his reserves up in contingents between September and 15 December, when the mobilization would be complete. MacArthur organized his forces into four commands: the North Luzon Force under Major General Jonathan Wainwright, which would be deployed in Luzon north of Manila; the South Luzon Force under Brigadier General George M Parker, Jr, which would defend the rest of the island; the Visayan-Mindanao Force under Brigadier General William F Sharp, which was supposed to defend the rest of the archipelago; and forces under Major General George F Moore, who commanded the harbor defenses in Manila and Subic Bays. A general reserve force including the Philippine Division of the US Army and the remaining Filipino division of the Philippine army was placed in an area around Manila. Wainwright, therefore, with little more than four ill-equipped and under-trained divisions had to defend an area about 300 miles long where the enemy attacks were expected. MacArthur ordered Wainwright not to withdraw from the beach positions which were to be held 'at all costs.' The artillery to be used was largely of World War I vintage, and artillery support was a small fraction of what was usual at the time and about one-third of the strength established for the Philippine Division. Motor vehicles, food and clothing were all scarce.

Right: A disconsolate MacArthur confers with Maj Gen Sutherland at the General's headquarters on Bataan in March 1942.

The continued optimism of Mac-Arthur, even in these last days, leads one to believe either that he did not know what was going on, which was doubtful, or that the staff knew and were afraid to tell MacArthur. This conclusion is dubious, however. MacArthur reports in his memoirs that he knew that he was short of material, but believed that the will of the Philippine people and the intensity of the resistance of his forces gave him a chance to hold the islands until reinforcements arrived

Below: MacArthur talks with Maj Gen Jonathan Wainwright in 1941. Wainwright stayed behind to surrender to the Japanese in 1942 and emerged a living skeleton at the end of the war.

from the States. It is certain that Mac-Arthur did not know the enormity of the problems facing his forces. It is more than likely that he had convinced himself that his luck would hold and that, somehow, the invincible image he had tirelessly constructed in the islands since 1935 was a true image of the man who could hold off any foe. MacArthur later blamed Washington for having let him down. He knew that Washington and particularly the President were of the opinion that the principal enemy was Germany, and that whatever crumbs he could expect after the fighting began would be insufficient to hold the islands for more than a few months, at most. It is more probable that he was deceiving

himself all along and, worst of all, deceiving the Philippine people.

Even at the last, political problems dogged MacArthur's footsteps. It had been proposed that MacArthur be given command of the naval forces in the area as well, but Admiral Thomas C Hart, commanding the US Asiatic Fleet, which consisted of three cruisers, plus some destroyers, submarines and small craft, insisted that these forces remain under his control. MacArthur objected vehemently, and relations between Hart and MacArthur deteriorated. Furthermore MacArthur still held out the hope that the Japanese would bypass the Philippines in order to avoid fighting the United States, and concentrate instead

Above: Japanese General Homma lands on Luzon in December 1941. His campaign to conquer the Philippines was masterly and swift.

on seizing British and Dutch possessions in Southeast Asia. Although historians now know that this idea was discussed in the presence of the Emperor it was rejected; it was not unrealistic of Mac-Arthur to have thought of this possibility, however.

MacArthur was also ordered not to initiate any action until the Japanese opened hostilities; the first overt moves were to come from the enemy. Therefore, it must have occurred to Roosevelt and Marshall that the Philippines might be bypassed. Roosevelt hoped that when the attack came, it would come on the Philippines because only a direct attack on American territory would fully convince the American public that America should go to war. This move was contemplated months before and it was for this reason that American naval power, such as it was, was almost completely recalled to Pearl Harbor, where the Americans felt it would be safe from Japanese attack. To have left the Ameri-

can Pacific Fleet in the Philippines without adequate air cover would have made it an open target when the Japanese attack came.

MacArthur could not have known that Roosevelt had given his word to the Dutch that if the Japanese attacked the Dutch East Indies alone, without hitting the Philippines, the United States would come to the aid of the Dutch. One thing is certain: the Japanese thought very little of MacArthur's defense schemes. Japanese intelligence, which was amazingly accurate, and which had been collected over several years by Japanese civilians operating within the islands as well as through the more usual channels, had a thorough knowledge of American strength in the Philippines. The Japanese Fourteenth Army was allotted only two divisions to accomplish its projected conquest of the Philippines. Lieutenant General Homma would have powerful naval cover and the support of some 500 planes. He was instructed to complete his conquest of the islands within 50 days, after which part of his forces would be deployed to help in the attack

on Java, one of Japan's principal targets. The Japanese estimate was pretty close to the mark, and in many respects was pessimistic; the forces which took the Philippines were not even needed on Java, which fell at almost the same time as the Commonwealth did. It just took a little longer than the Japanese planned.

The question which remains is this: was MacArthur set up for a defeat? Of course, it is unthinkable that the President of the United States would wilfully desire American territory to fall into the hands of the enemy. Every indication is that Roosevelt and his generals in Washington had no choice but to accept the inevitable. American public opinion, even on the eve of war, was not fully convinced of the dangers which Germany and Japan posed to the security of the United States. It is also likely that Roosevelt was not anxious to have a victorious MacArthur on his hands; win the war he would; but the glory would not go to MacArthur. There could be no glory in an unsuccessful holding operation, and this was the role set out for MacArthur, whether he wanted it or not.

3:THE WARRIOR DEFEATED

In late November 1941 MacArthur received reports from Admiral Hart and General Marshall that there was little prospect that an agreement would be reached with Japan and that Japanese troop movements indicated the likelihood of an attack in any direction. It was clear that an overt attack could take place at any moment, but MacArthur was again warned not to make the first move, but that this should not be construed to mean that MacArthur should not do everything in his power to make the island ready for attack short of making a preemptive strike himself. On 28 November the Navy Department sent the commanders of the Pacific and Asiatic Fleets a 'war warning' which stated that an aggressive move by Japan was to be expected within the next few days. MacArthur cabled Marshall telling him that everything was in readiness. Reports that Japanese ships were moving toward Malaya and unidentified aircraft appearing over Luzon strengthened this belief. MacArthur ordered Wainwright to be ready at any moment. It was expected that if an attack occurred on American territory it would be on the Philippines.

At 0330 on the morning (Philippine time) of 8 December General Sutherland heard over the radio that Pearl Harbor was being attacked by Japanese planes. He telephoned MacArthur at once, but it was not until two hours later that MacArthur was officially informed that America was at war with Japan, although at 0340 he had received a telephone call from Washington informing him that Japan had attacked Hawaii. MacArthur's first impression was that Japan would suffer a serious defeat at Pearl Harbor. He awaited reports of a simultaneous attack on the Philippines.

There was only one radar station operative in the islands. At 0930 reconnaissance planes reported a force of

Left: A mopping-up campaign on Bougainville in the Solomons after MacArthur took over command of the Southwest Pacific Theater.

enemy bombers over Lingayen Gulf heading toward Manila. Brereton ordered pursuit planes up to intercept them, but the enemy bombers veered off without making contact with the Americans. Instead they turned north and attacked Baguio, the summer capital, and other targets. MacArthur was still under the impression that Japan had suffered a setback at Pearl Harbor, and concluded that the Japanese planes veered off because they had received word of a Japanese defeat. Sometime between 0930 and 1130 however, MacArthur learned the truth; much to his astonishment, the Japanese had achieved a smashing victory over American forces in Hawaii, who were taken by surprise despite the warnings given.

At 1145 MacArthur received a report that an overpowering enemy formation of planes was closing in on Clark Field, America's principal air base in the islands. America had only two airfields which could handle the big B-17 bombers, which were MacArthur's only really strong card: Clark Field, north of Manila, and Del Monte, 800 miles to the south in Mindanao. Two of the four squadrons of B-17s had been removed to Del Monte some days before the war broke out in order to keep them out of danger. The rest were on the ground at Clark. Brereton proposed that these B-17s be sent into the air at once to make a strike against Japanese Formosa. This proposal was put to MacArthur on three occasions on the morning of the 8th, but MacArthur refused to act in each instance. From 0800 onward the bombers were in the air but without any bombs. MacArthur ordered an attack on Formosa for the afternoon, so at 1130 the bombers were back on the ground at Clark being armed. The Japanese planes, however, the main force consisting of 108 bombers and 84 Zeros (fighter planes), were delayed by fog from taking off from Formosa, and did not leave until 1015. Within an hour and a half they were over Clark and Iba Fields. When the attack was over the United States had lost 18 of its 35 B-17s in the Philippines,

53 fighters and 25–30 other aircraft. Only seven Japanese fighters had been lost in the attack.

There can be little doubt that MacArthur lost the Philippines in the first hours of the war. Had the bombers taken off armed from Clark at once, they could have made a strike against Formosa before the Japanese were in the air with their main strike force. MacArthur later denied any knowledge of the fact that Brereton had made the proposal that the American bombers take off for Formosa immediately. He claimed that the proposals had been made to Sutherland, not to him, and that they should have been made to him. It would be useless to try to place blame in this way. The fact remains that MacArthur was in charge and, even if the proposals had not been made to him personally, he should have thought of the idea and, at least, done something to protect his only really effective weapon, his bombers.

MacArthur argued later that the bombers would have had insufficient fighter cover, and that the effort, if made, would have been suicidal. Yet he did authorize the bombers to leave in the afternoon, after the fog over Formosa had lifted and after the enemy planes had already made their way to the Philippines. Even if he had not decided to send the bombers to Formosa, he could at least have flown them to Del Monte, where they could have been used later on. Their flight over the Philippines unarmed, only to return to Clark to be armed, was futile. It was a disastrous error on MacArthur's part, for which he and the American forces were to pay dearly. After the morning of the 8th, it was clear that the Americans had lost the Philippines, and what was to occur subsequently was merely a tragic epilogue to the initial error.

It still might be mentioned in MacArthur's defense that his directive from Washington specifically stated that he should make no overt move against the enemy until they had done so first. Therefore, this would seem to preclude a strike against Formosa. But since Japanese planes were sighted over Luzon

at 0930, the order to strike could have been given at that time. There could be little doubt that the United States was at war with Japan after news came in the early morning hours that Pearl Harbor had been attacked. What further incentive did MacArthur need?

Perhaps a strike against Formosa might have made some difference in the long-term result; it might have delayed the Japanese for a while. The overwhelming air and naval superiority which Japan had could not have been repelled in the long run. The initial air raids on Luzon were followed by Japanese landings at points somewhat remote from Manila: Aparri and Vigan in the north on 10 December and Legaspi in the south on the 12th. MacArthur thought that these landings were made with the idea of establishing airfields from which to cover other major landings which were to be made later on. Japanese confidence was high, and they felt they could take the islands with a small number of men landing from Formosa in the north and from Palau Island in the south.

MacArthur believed that he could last for a considerable period as long as reinforcements which he counted on were forthcoming. Back in Washington the War Department was shaken by the disastrous news from Pearl Harbor. Most of the Pacific Fleet had been

Below: The remains of an American submarine in the port of Cavite, the Philippines. The USN forces at Cavite were decimated in the early Japanese air strikes in December 1941.

destroyed at a stroke. Roosevelt and Stimson were not of a mind to send what remaining forces they had 3–4000 miles from their forward base, against what they knew to be superior enemy forces, just to save MacArthur's skin in the Philippines. The islands, in their view, were not worth the effort based on the strength which America then had. But MacArthur felt that the navy could and should deliver a counteroffensive against Japan immediately. He suggested a bold stroke which might have had some effect: to send a group of carriers against the home islands which would force Japan to withdraw from the areas they were now attacking. This move certainly would have raised morale in the Philippines and the States, but whether it would have been successful or not is another matter. Moving imaginary fleets across a map may create a smug atmosphere at headquarters, but such actions are pointless when one cannot deliver the goods. The only two capital ships the Allies had in the Western Pacific, the British battleship *Prince of Wales* and its sister battlecruiser *Repulse*, were sunk off the Malayan coast on 10 December; without sufficient air cover they were sitting targets for the Japanese.

MacArthur still believed reinforcements would be sent. In fact a convoy of seven vessels escorted by the cruiser *Pensacola* was on its way to Manila when the war broke out. The convoy was carrying a field artillery brigade with 20 75mm guns, 18 P-40s, 52 A-24 dive bombers and con-

Above: The Japanese landing at Lingayen Gulf during their conquest of the Philippines. American and Filipino defenses were so weak that they were forced to surrender most of the archipelago almost immediately.

siderable supplies of ammunition. On 12 December the convoy was rerouted to Brisbane. MacArthur complained bitterly to Hart about this, but Hart, according to MacArthur, was of the opinion that the Philippines were doomed. At roughly this time MacArthur also asked for 250 dive bombers and 300 fighters which, he suggested, could be flown in from aircraft carriers. Marshall assured him that some aircraft would be sent to the Philippines, but the bulk would go to Brisbane. By 13 December MacArthur was telling Marshall that the decision to concentrate the war effort on Germany first should be reversed and that all available reinforcements should be used against Japan. This course of action was rejected, of course, and none of the *Pensacola* convoy's men or material ever got to the Philippines. Although two vessels were sent forward from Brisbane, they were diverted to Darwin later.

MacArthur showed a complete lack of understanding of America's capabilities at this time, and disagreed violently with her 'Europe first' policy, as he always had done. The brilliant tactician and leader of men of World War I was politically out of touch with his government and most of his fellow senior generals. Although American public opinion was shocked and em-

bittered by the Pearl Harbor disaster, only a few die-hard remnants of the America-First, quasi-isolationist clique still supported a 'defeat Japan first' policy. MacArthur, though out of touch with the United States for some time, could have surmised this, but he was so wrapped up in his own affairs that he lost sight of America's primary objective. Worst of all, his tactical ability failed him, and his overestimation of America's present strength caused him to ask the Chief of Staff for equipment that America could not spare.

The mobilization of Filipino manpower, however, was a success. By 8 December it was almost complete and some units were even overstrength; new units were formed out of the surplus, including two regiments and two battalions of artillery. Despite this strength in manpower, MacArthur recognized on the 12th that his original plan of defending the whole of the archipelago could not be accomplished. He informed President Quezon that if the Japanese landed in strength he would concentrate his forces on the Bataan Peninsula outside Manila and withdraw his headquarters and the government to Corregidor at the tip of the peninsula; in short, that he was returning to War Plan Orange which had been the accepted one until four months before. This would mean that Manila would be declared an open city. It was probably at this point that MacArthur began to realize that the game was up and that the only effect resistance would have would be to delay the

inevitable Japanese victory. MacArthur was then faced with the task of transporting quantities of ammunition and food to Bataan to prepare for the siege, to withdraw his Luzon forces into the peninsula, and to establish a defensive position across the neck of Bataan. MacArthur, however, delayed the decision to withdraw to Bataan until after the main Japanese landings had taken place, thereby losing further time and postponing what he knew had to be done. Again indecision and bad timing were to cost the Americans and Filipinos heavily.

General Terauchi's Southern Area Army had been charged with the attack on Allied-held Southeast Asia. Four armies were organized for the assault, one of which, the Fourteenth, composed of two divisions, one brigade and one regimental group, was ear-marked to take the Philippines. Lieutenant General Homma's Fourteenth Army included the 48th Division, two of whose regiments were Formosan, and the 16th Division. One of the Formosan regiments had made the initial landing in northern Luzon while two battalions of the 16th Division, plus a battalion of marines, had made the first landing in southern Luzon. Homma, therefore, had four infantry regiments left. He sent three of these and two regiments of tanks to Lingayen Gulf and the rest to the south.

At first glance this force did not seem formidable opposition to the defenders who had at least nine divisions under arms. But the lack of naval reinforcements and air power was to make all the difference. The main Japanese force was to land along a 20-mile front and then fan out northward to link with the forces already on Luzon. MacArthur had expected an attack at about this spot within two weeks of the decision being made to withdraw to Bataan; that is, on or about 28 December. At dawn on the 22nd the invasion began in a storm which caused the loss of many landing craft. The second wave of landing forces was also delayed, but once ashore made short work of the ill-trained Philippine troops. There was no successful American bombardment of the landing, and General Homma decided to press forward against the advice of some of his staff. MacArthur's hopes that, despite their lack of training the Filipino troops could put up a stalwart

Below: The USS *Pensacola* was one of the few ships of the American fleet in the Western Pacific in early December 1941.

Inset: A P-40 Warhawk of the type used by the Flying Tigers in the CBI Theater. Few were available for the defense of the Philippines. Eighteen were sent in a convoy escorted by *Pensacola* but were diverted to Brisbane.

defense, were dashed from the outset. He reported that they had broken at the first appearance of the enemy. The 71st Division, despite some reinforcements, fled the following day from their position across the Rosario road, which was to block the route toward the south and Manila. That same day Wainwright received permission to withdraw behind the Agno River, which crossed the Japanese route to Manila. If Wainwright could hold this position for any length of time, the Bataan fortress could complete its preparations and acquire sufficient supplies to maintain itself even under a long and heavy siege. MacArthur wisely sent most of his well-trained Philippine Division to Bataan at this stage. By this time Marshall had approved MacArthur's plan to declare Manila an open city and to withdraw to the peninsula.

On Christmas Day Admiral Hart left the Philippines to join his main force, which had already left and was now in the Dutch East Indies. Brereton was now in Darwin with his bomber force. All that was left of the remaining naval forces were six motor torpedo boats, a few other small vessels and a few

submarines, which were soon to leave as well. In little more than two weeks MacArthur's high hopes for defending the islands had collapsed; MacArthur and Wainwright were left to stave off the inevitable with little more than a brave band of American troops and indifferent support from their paper army of Philippine soldiers.

On 24 December the Japanese invasion of southern Luzon met with equal success. By the end of their first day the Japanese had crossed the island and were prepared to move north and westward toward Manila. Unless Wainwright's line could hold, Manila would be surrounded. By Christmas night Wainwright had been pushed back to the Agno River. The American lines held for two nights, as the Japanese awaited the arrival of more artillery. By the 28th

Above: Japanese tanks enter Manila after its declaration as an open city. Manila could not be defended and the US forces had to retire the Bataan Peninsula.

the defenders had given up their first two positions and were back to their last lines of defense. MacArthur, who reported that his men were tired but still had the situation well in hand, was forced to supply them by using commercial buses and private motor vehicles, as there were not enough military vehicles to do the job. Wainwright was still told to hang on as long as he could and then withdraw, while the engineers dynamited bridges and roads as they retreated.

General Homma, however, upset the American plans by attempting to cut across to block the retreat into Bataan, but he had been ordered to take Manila, despite the fact that he knew that MacArthur himself had already gone to Corregidor. Instead of pressing on toward Bataan, he sent the bulk of his forces toward Manila and only sent a

regimental group toward Bataan. This move allowed the Americans to continue their withdrawal. Meanwhile, the main contingents of the South Luzon Force were hurriedly making their way northward, and within seven days had withdrawn 140 miles through very rugged country. The rearguard which was holding the roads along the retreat route made a sharp counteroffensive which cost the Japanese eight tanks and which thereafter slowed their advance. By 1 January most of the organized units of troops were either in Bataan or near San Fernando on the road back. Homma's army pressed toward an undefended Manila, which was taken on the following day.

The rearguard made its way to Bataan within the next five days, harassed by Japanese forces as it withdrew. The withdrawal had not been unsuccessful, but 13,000 troops were lost in the process, most of them deserters: dispirited Filipinos from Wainwright's force. The supply buildup on Bataan, however, was less successful. The war

plans had called for supplies for 43,000 men for six months, but, due to MacArthur's delay in issuing the order to retreat to Bataan, this was not achieved. Corregidor had rations for 10,000 men for six months, but Bataan had only enough for 100,000 men for 30 days. The crowded and chaotic conditions in the beleaguered peninsula called for more than even the war plans had foreseen. There were not 43,000 men there now, but 80,000, and there were over 25,000 civilian refugees. Before the last troops entered the fortress MacArthur reduced the daily rations to half their normal amount for civilians and soldiers alike, about 2000 calories.

Homma's troops were to be reduced because of orders received which asked him to release his best group, the 48th Division, for action in Java, which according to the original Japanese time-

Right: A Japanese wartime picture magazine portraying an American flag, helmet and rifle abandoned during the fighting on Luzon.

寫眞
週報

輯　編　局　報　情
ン七十・號八十百二第・日九廿月四

table was not to be invaded for at least another month. Japan now felt confident enough to ship these forces southward and replace them with the six battalions of the 65th Brigade. In opposition to this reduced Japanese force MacArthur still had two regular Philippine army divisions and seven Philippine army reserve divisions, which, if they could have been given reinforcements or even enough food and ammunition, could have held out for quite some time. The assumption MacArthur continued to make, that the United States could send fresh supplies, was unrealistic. Once Japan controlled the seas and air, it would be suicidal for the United States to risk reinforcing Bataan when the Dutch East Indies were still insecure. When Singapore fell even this would have little effect. MacArthur later blamed Marshall for not having come through with the supplies he had promised. He asked Washington repeatedly for help but no help was forthcoming. MacArthur blamed the lack of a will-to-win in Washington for his defeat. This cannot be accepted as the real reason. Admiral Hart gave the Dutch East Indies higher priority than the Philippines; it had tin and rubber which was vital to Japanese as well as American interests, not to mention its oil. With limited supplies available to the Americans, priorities had to be made, no matter how valiant and futile the effort then being made in the Philippines seemed.

On 10 January MacArthur received a message from the Commander in Chief of the Japanese Expeditionary Force. Homma told MacArthur that he was 'well aware that you are doomed. The end is near. The question is how long you will be able to resist. You have already cut rations by half. I appreciate the fighting spirit of yourself and your troops who have been fighting with courage. Your prestige and honor have been upheld. However, in order to avoid needless bloodshed and to save the remnants of your divisions and your auxiliary troops, you are advised to surrender.' When MacArthur failed to answer this note, the Japanese showered Bataan with leaflets asking the soldiers to surrender despite what it called MacArthur's 'stupid refusal' to accept surrender proposals. Japan implored the Filipinos to surrender at once and

Above: Japanese light tank in operation in the Philippines. The Japanese tanks were of a poor quality mitigated by the lack of sufficient artillery to combat them.

'build your new Philippines for and by Filipinos.' These attempts were falling on largely deaf ears mainly because of the Filipinos' faith in the Americans granting independence to them at an early date. The concept of a Philippine Commonwealth had paid off.

MacArthur refused to give up for two reasons. First, he was not the sort of man to surrender without a severe struggle. Second, he still expected the promised supplies to come from the States. Marshall undoubtedly made a mistake when he encouraged MacArthur's hopes, which did not have a prayer of being fulfilled. When President Roosevelt broadcast to the Philippine people on 28 December that the United States Navy 'is following an intensive and well-planned campaign against Japa-

nese forces which will result in positive assistance to the defense of the Philippine Islands,' he was leading the Filipinos up the garden path. They still had faith in MacArthur's word and the word of President Roosevelt, and the disillusionment that followed was all the greater for these assurances having been made. However, it must be added that MacArthur had begged Roosevelt to give the Filipinos something to go on, and the President's message was largely inspired by MacArthur's insistence that some words of encouragement ought to be made. Again, the lack of political expertise on MacArthur's part was to injure his cause. There was no hope of MacArthur receiving any aid. Brigadier General Eisenhower told Marshall as early as 10 December that it would be a long time before any major reinforcements could be sent to the Philippines and that therefore America's major base had to be Australia. Marshall agreed with this assessment. Nothing was to

be gained by holding out false hopes to MacArthur's forces on the Bataan Peninsula.

Misinformation of another sort was to further affect MacArthur's judgment of the situation. He believed that Japan had six divisions in the Philippines, not two. By passing this misinformation on to Washington, it was no wonder that the Americans had given up the fight for the islands. However, Homma was equally misinformed. He thought that the Americans had only about 25,000 men on Bataan, when they actually had over three times that number. Homma therefore assigned the siege of Bataan to the inexperienced 65th Brigade and a regiment from the 16th Division – only nine battalions in all, plus artillery and a tank regiment. The invasion plan was to advance two columns, one on either side of the peninsula.

By underestimating the Americans' strength, the Japanese were going to run into fierce and unexpected opposi-

tion. The attack, which began on 9 January, started off badly. When the Japanese were beaten back by a regiment of Philippine Scouts on the 11th, Major General Akira Nara, in charge of the 65th Brigade, realized that he was going to face far stronger resistance than he expected, despite the attempts of 'Tokyo Rose' to weaken the Filipinos' and Americans' resolve through her nightly broadcasts to the troops. Brigadier General George Parker, however, had been thrown back from the hills, and MacArthur's inland flank was exposed. On the 15th MacArthur sent another message to his troops, urging them to fight on because 'help is on the way from the United States. Thousands of troops and hundreds of planes are being dispatched. . . . It is imperative that our troops hold until these reinforcements arrive. No further retreat is possible.' That MacArthur believed every word he said makes the situation even more tragic in retrospect.

Above: A motorcycle dispatch rider tries to take a quick nap on Bataan, with his weapons ready for immediate action in case the American position was overrun by surprise.

Parker's men slowly withdrew after intense fighting while the Japanese carried out a similar maneuver in Wainwright's inland flank. By the 22nd MacArthur had ordered Sutherland to withdraw to a new line of defense. The Japanese had suffered heavy casualties in this 16-day battle, losing over 1400 men, and were now faced with a shorter and stronger line, from Bagac to Orion. The Americans also repelled, with some difficulty, a seaborne attack on the southwest coast of the peninsula. The first Japanese thrusts against the Bagac-Orion line were repelled, and for a fortnight, despite heavy bombardment, the Japanese were unable to break through. At the same time the Japanese had been shelling Corregidor, where MacArthur kept his headquarters now, so much so that the original and rather exposed offices and quarters were abandoned for the safety of tunnels, where MacArthur's command was to continue its operations. Many of his men, especially those closest to him, were impressed by his *sang froid* and calm demeanor in the face of disaster. This view, however, was not always shared by the men in the field, who called him 'Dugout Doug,'

since he had not emerged from Corregidor for weeks while the fierce fighting continued on Bataan. This unjust ballad was composed:

Dugout Doug MacArthur lies,
a'shaking on the Rock
Safe from all the bombers and
from any sudden shock.

This was hardly fair, since the Rock was under heavy and almost constant

bombardment, and MacArthur sometimes went out of his tunnel-HQ to brave the hideous cacophony and terror which destroyed everything standing above ground. MacArthur disdained wearing a protective helmet and was almost killed on more than one occasion when shrapnel and bombs tore through the place where he was standing.

Philippine morale, despite MacArthur's efforts, was flagging. General Aguinaldo, hero of the Spanish-American War, wrote MacArthur begging him to give up the fight in order to save lives which would be lost for nothing. MacArthur admitted being shaken by this message. On 8 February President Quezon sent a message to Roosevelt through Marshall asking that the United States grant independence immediately to the Philippines, that the islands be neutralized, and that both American and Japanese forces be withdrawn. MacArthur sent an accompanying message, admitting that his men were exhausted and that 'complete destruction' might come at any time. Roosevelt replied that although he could not promise immediate aid, 'every ship at our disposal is bringing to the southwest Pacific the forces which will ultimately smash the invader' and MacArthur was urged to fight on to the end by FDR. The President added that if it were possible Quezon and his ministers should be flown to America via Australia. Quezon broadcast further appeals to his people and the fight went on, although Roosevelt authorized MacArthur to negotiate a capitulation if necessary. The timing would be left to MacArthur. MacArthur replied, 'I have not the slightest intention in the world of surrendering or capitulating the Filipino forces of my command. I intend to fight to destruction on Bataan and then do the same on Corregidor.' Marshall suggested that MacArthur's wife and young son be evacuated by submarine, and Quezon begged MacArthur to accept the offer. After conferring with his wife, MacArthur told Quezon, 'she will stay with me to the end. We drink from the same cup'. He told Marshall; 'I and my family will share the fate of the garrison.' Quezon, deeply moved, himself left soon

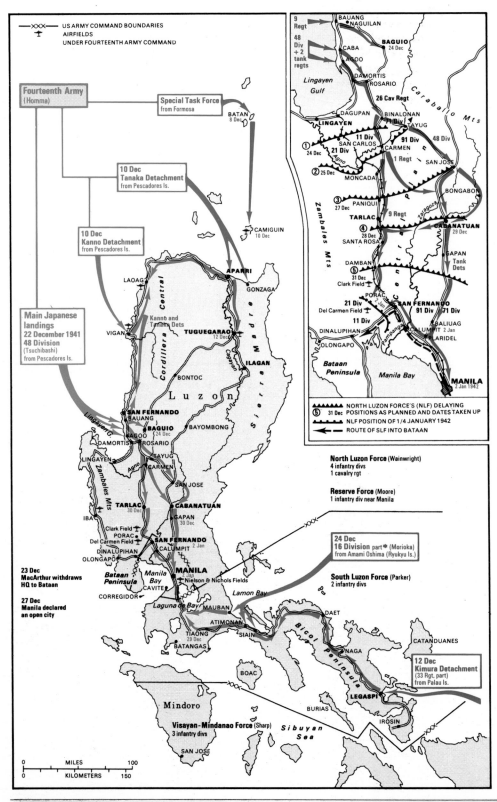

Left: The swift Japanese conquest of Luzon, the main island of the Philippines. The inset depicts the withdrawal to Bataan.

after and slipped his signet ring on MacArthur's finger before he went with his family, telling him 'When they find your body, I want them to know you fought for my country.'

On 16 February MacArthur ordered yet another assault on the enemy forces. On the 22nd, as the Japanese slowly pressed forward, MacArthur was ordered to go to Mindanao for not more than a week, after which he would be appointed to take command of all the Allied forces in the Southwest Pacific with his headquarters in Australia. MacArthur later reported that his first reaction was simply to resign his commission and enlist as a soldier to stay with his men. On the 24th, persuaded by his staff officers that he should follow the directive, he replied that he would go but he would pick the right time in order to sustain flagging morale. He said that 15

Below: Japanese forces landing on the island of Corregidor, which dominated Manila Bay. The American and Philippine defense was brave but hopeless against formidable, even overwhelming odds.

March would probably be the right time. Homma's forces, however, had slackened their pressure on the peninsula, and on 9 March he was replaced by General Yamashita, who had just taken Singapore. The lull on Bataan had lasted for three weeks and MacArthur decided that this was the right time to leave. Not waiting for the submarine, which was due to pick him up on the 15th, he and his family as well as some of his staff went to Mindanao in torpedo boats. They left Corregidor on 12 March and reached Mindanao on the 14th.

There was a good deal of scurrilous gossip floating around Corregidor that MacArthur had taken along phonographs, his collection of books and other personal items of value rather than taking more men with him. MacArthur denied this categorically. Yet there is still some evidence to support at least some of the gossip. Even if the story is completely without foundation, the fact that many of his men even now swear to the fact that the gossip is true is an indication of the sort of rapport MacArthur had

with the majority of his men on the fortress island. Although most of those closest to him attest to his bravery in a crisis and his loyalty to his men, the majority of those in the field did not share this opinion. If MacArthur's motto had been to lead from the front in World War I, his reputation was that of one who led from the rear and deserted in the face of the enemy when the chips were down at Bataan. Despite the fact that much if not all of this was unfair and untrue, inasmuch as the Commander in Chief, Roosevelt, ordered him to go to Australia, one cannot overlook the comments of men who were to go to enemy prison camp for years as a result of the loss of the Philippines, and even the unfortunates who fell in the infamous March of Death to the camps after Corregidor fell. When Wainwright finally surrendered on 6 May, after a long and bitter fight that cost the enemy thousands of lives and the Americans and Filipinos thousands more, an estimated 140,000 men became prisoners of the Japanese throughout the archipelago.

Above: Japanese troops lower the American flag in the last redoubt, Corregidor, after its fall in May 1942. General Wainwright surrendered his forces into Japanese hands. By that time MacArthur was safely in Australia after his near-miraculous seaborne escape.

Right: Three American soldiers on the Death March after the surrender. Thousands of US and Philippine troops died on their long march into captivity, when they were denied food and rest. The weak were left to die.

The extravagant praise given MacArthur for his defense of the Philippines by members of his staff does not hold up under scrutiny. Despite the fact that money was scarce and materials for war were in short supply, MacArthur could still have done more to prepare the Philippines in the six years he had before the war broke out. The troops were painfully unready and MacArthur did not fully realize how unprepared they were. Although his errors on the morning of 8 December were not crucial to the loss of the Philippines, which probably would have been lost anyway, he should have realized that without sea and air superiority or even parity he had no chance of winning or preventing the Japanese from doing so. By continually promising his men and the Filipino public that help was coming, implying that this help would come imminently, MacArthur betrayed the faith of those who believed in him.

While on Bataan and Corregidor his failure to create a rapport with his frontline troops did not help morale. Even the long fight which the Japanese had to endure to take the peninsula cannot really be attributed to MacArthur's planning or strategy. The fact that Homma was replaced in mid-campaign and that the Japanese army was weakened by the withdrawal of their best troops to other areas accounts more for the long delay in the fall of Corregidor than any effort of MacArthur's, although the valiance of those who defended the peninsula cannot be questioned. Although the siege of Bataan cost the Japanese lives and tied down some of their troops, it tied down more American troops and cost the Americans and Filipinos more. By the time MacArthur reached Australia on the morning of 17 March, the Battle of the Java Sea had already been lost and the Dutch East Indies had been taken by the Japanese. Southeast Asia was theirs and the fighting on Bataan, for the Japanese anyway, was only a mopping-up campaign. They could have taken Bataan and Corregidor sooner if they had not put first things first and placed the Indies and Singapore as the top priorities in the area.

Sir Edward Grey used to say, 'fine words butter no parsnips.' All of MacArthur's baroque prose during and after the event could not disguise the fact that the United States had suffered a crushing

Above: General Sir Thomas Blamey greets MacArthur after his landing at the airfield near Port Moresby, New Guinea. MacArthur was first evacuated by boat through Japanese-dominated sea lanes.

defeat in the Philippines and the Western Pacific. However, MacArthur's reputation at home in the States was enhanced by his noble phrases. Roosevelt found, to his surprise, that MacArthur emerged out of one of America's most stunning defeats as a hero in spite of himself; the fate of the beleaguered troops in Bataan touched a chord in the hearts of patriotic Americans, incensed by the surprise attack on Pearl Harbor and the heavy losses America and the Allies were suffering in the first months of 1942. Roosevelt, sensing this, saw that MacArthur's propaganda value was useful to the American war effort. When asked by reporters for a statement when he arrived in Australia, MacArthur, weary from the difficult journey, casually remarked, 'The President of the United States ordered me to break through the Japanese lines and proceed from Corregidor to Australia for the purpose, as I understand it, of organizing the American offensive against Japan, a primary object of which is the relief of the Philippines. I came through and I shall return.' This last phrase became a symbol of continued American resistance to Japan to both the Philippine and American public; MacArthur was awarded the Medal of Honor for his role in the Philippines.

After MacArthur arrived in Australia members of his staff flew to Melbourne,

but MacArthur was met in Alice Springs in the interior of the country by Patrick J Hurley, who told him that every generation of Americans had its hero: Pershing, Dewey, Lindbergh; 'America,' he said, 'had now taken MacArthur to their hearts as its hero.' Music to MacArthur's ears, this praise was mitigated by the news MacArthur also received: there were only about 25,000 American troops in Australia and only 260 aircraft, many of them unusable. Panicky Australians suggested that the Allies withdraw to a Brisbane Line which would leave the whole of the north coast open to Japanese seizure. Although most reports that historians have at their disposal now indicate that the Japanese intended to consolidate their enormous gains and deal with Australia later, this was not known at the time. MacArthur was stunned by the news, and assured the Labour Prime Minister of Australia, John Curtin, that he would handle the front if Curtin took care of the rear. Curtin gave MacArthur unqualified support. MacArthur's receipt of the American Medal of Honor encouraged him and tended to put those rumours to rest which indicated that Marshall and MacArthur were not getting along. They were not, of course, and the situation was not made any better when, later in the year, MacArthur refused Marshall's suggestion that poor General Wainwright, then in captivity after the Death March, be granted the same honor.

MacArthur attended a meeting of the Advisory War Council in Canberra late in March, a body which was composed of members of the Australian ministry and members of the opposition, and told the body that he doubted whether Japan would press on to invade Australia right away. MacArthur assumed correctly that Japan was over-extended and would only try to bomb northern Australian ports and perhaps to seize them but to go no further. He therefore rejected the idea of a Brisbane Line. He again insisted that the Allies concentrate on defeating Japan first rather than Germany, which as usual, ran counter to the accepted view and was not likely to gain a sympathetic ear in Washington, which, after all, was the ultimate authority for sending whatever supplies could be spared to the Pacific. MacArthur continued to harp on this theme throughout the rest of the war and therefore intensified the animosity felt toward him among many in high places in the United States. Such continued opposition on MacArthur's part was counterproductive and even less likely to yield the desired results than a policy of acquiescence, or, at least, sullen silence. Roosevelt was not wholly opposed to sending supplies to Mac-Arthur's theater of operations. Admiral King supported MacArthur's view in front of the President, but a policy of aiding Britain first remained the highest priority. At one stage Roosevelt was inclined to give MacArthur the 100,000

Below: The aircraft carrier USS *Lexington* on 8 May 1942 during the Battle of the Coral Sea. *Lexington* was sunk during the battle but the Japanese plan to attack Port Moresby was frustrated.

combat troops he asked for as well as the 1000 planes, but he was finally persuaded that this was inadvisable, since it was generally felt that the build up in Britain must not be slowed down whatever compelling reasons might be argued.

During the first few months in Australia MacArthur was a bitterly disappointed man. Not only had he just been defeated but the immediate prospects of making a return to the Philippines were dimming. Although the United States had begun an extraordinarily successful build up of troops and material, by mid-1942 America was clearly not fully tooled up for war. American industry had stopped production of most consumer goods by this time, but retooling of factories and converting them into war plants was not and could not be an overnight operation. MacArthur did not quite understand the problems of creating an army and a war machine within the United States and was, perhaps understandably, impatient at what he considered procrastinations and bureaucratic incompetence. While MacArthur was in the Philippines decisions had been made to send men to the Pacific theater of operations, and many did go to India, Java and elsewhere. In fact, 57,000 got to Australia by mid-1942 and 79,000 were sent to the Pacific area as a whole, far more, in fact, than went to Britain and the European theater of operations in the first months of that year. MacArthur had little to complain about considering the circumstances, but complain he did nevertheless.

A few days before he reached Australia

the decision had been reached to reorganize the Allied commands which had already undergone several reorganization schemes already. There would be three main theaters of operations: the Pacific, directed by the American Joint Chiefs of Staff; the Indian Ocean and Middle East, directed by the British Chiefs of Staff; and the European-Atlantic, under the joint responsibility of Britain and America. The Pacific theater was divided into two main areas: the Pacific Ocean, including the Central, South and North Pacific Areas; and the Southwest Pacific, including Australia, New Guinea, the Philippines and most of the Indies. On 1 April MacArthur was ordered to hold the key military bases of Australia 'as bases for future offensive action.' Orders henceforth were to come through the American Joint Chiefs of Staff. On 18 April he assumed command of all Allied forces in the Southwest Pacific and his immediate subordinates were announced. Of his senior staff, which was appointed the next day, only three members had not come with MacArthur from the Philippines. Although urged by Marshall to do so, MacArthur resolutely refused to make room for Dutch and Australian officers to serve on his senior staff. Furthermore, most of his staff was drawn from the ranks of the US Army, rather than from all three services. His headquarters team was entirely drawn from the American army, and the naval, land and air headquarters were housed separately. As a result MacArthur was not in close contact with air and naval

experts. His immediate subordinates, General Sir Thomas Blamey, Major General George H Brett and Vice Admiral Herbert F Leary, for example, did have representatives of all the Allies working under them, and therefore they created more the sort of command which MacArthur ought to have created on his own team. MacArthur, plagued by his feelings of isolation and neglect, had decided to draw around him the small and devoted staff who had served him for so long and was not happy about diluting it with outsiders.

The naval and air forces at Mac-Arthur's command at that time were meager indeed: a few cruisers and submarines and a considerable number of smaller vessels of the Australian navy. However, MacArthur was anxious to strike a counteroffensive at once. Mac-Arthur's first directive relating to a general plan came on 25 April when he told the Allied land forces not to allow any Japanese landing on the northeast coast of Australia or the southwest coast of Australian-held New Guinea. This was short of an all-out offensive against New Guinea, but it was a positive step taken to ensure that the whole of the island did not fall into enemy hands.

By this time Corregidor had fallen and Port Moresby in New Guinea had been fortified with planes and a brigade of militia to support the small Papuan battalion. At Darwin, on Australia proper, a group of about 15,000 troops awaited the Japanese onslaught and three US fighter squadrons were also ready to help in the defense. It was at this point that the Japanese planned the next stage of their offensive: a seaborne expedition mounted at Rabaul and aimed for Port Moresby. The Americans, prepared for this offensive through the interception of decoded Japanese signals, concentrated a naval force in the Solomon Sea which included two carriers. Although the engagements on 5–8 May cost the Allies the loss of the *Lexington*, an aircraft carrier, as well as two other vessels, a small Japanese carrier was sunk and, more important, the Japanese were turned back. This stalemate was actually a victory inasmuch as the force in Port Moresby probably would not have been able to withstand concentrated Japanese pressure. By now there were only two undamaged American aircraft carriers in the Pacific and the

Above: MacArthur inspects the troops of the 9th Australian Division at Atherton Tablelands in Queensland. MacArthur was to take all Australian forces under his command to build up a new Allied army.

Americans had reason to believe that Japan was about to attack Hawaii.

On 12 May MacArthur told Curtin that the situation was bad and, furthermore, had already pressed Marshall for two carriers, three divisions and an increase in his air force. These continual messages were not going to change Washington's Hitler-first policy very much and served merely as an annoyance. There was little MacArthur could do at this stage except to send comforting messages to Wainwright until Corregidor fell and issue press releases which, admittedly, did much to sustain morale in the States. For example, he remarked that 'Corregidor needs no comment from me. It has sounded its own story at the mouth of its guns. It has scrolled its

own epitaph on enemy tablets, but through the bloody haze of its last reverberating shots, I shall always seem to see the vision of its grim, gaunt and ghostly men, still unafraid.' Purple prose notwithstanding Wainwright was still not recommended for the Medal of Honor.

On 25 May MacArthur indicated that he expected a renewed attack on Port Moresby and therefore reinforced the town as well as sending units to forward positions in Queensland. Soon afterward, however, the great Japanese onslaught in the Central Pacific, long expected, took place, and in the Battle of Midway the Japanese carrier force suffered a stunning setback, the first major Allied victory of the war in the Pacific. Stirred by the victory MacArthur again implored Marshall for more men and weapons so as to capture the Japanese base at Rabaul and force the enemy back to his base on the island of Truk, 700 miles further north. He needed an

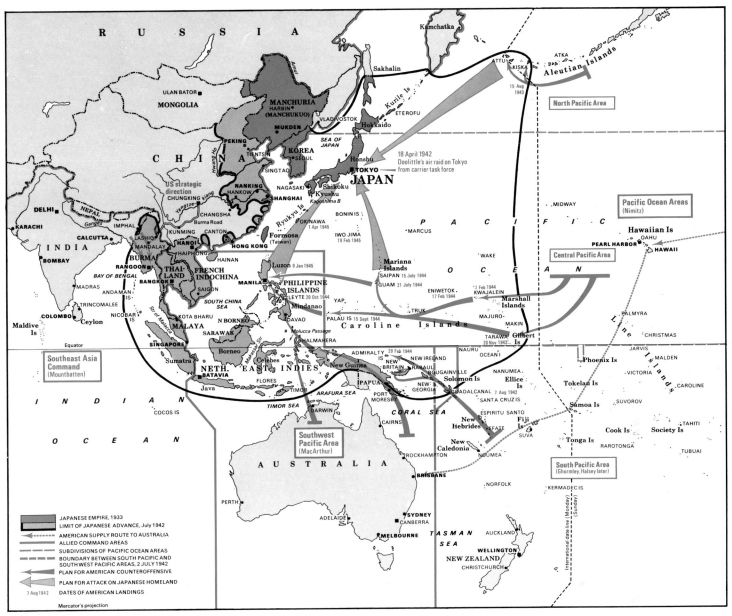

amphibious division and at least two carriers plus a substantial naval force. There were serious objections to this plan. First of all, the carriers would be exposed to attack from enemy land-based aircraft, while at the same time Allied land-based aircraft could not protect the fleet. An army man to the fingernails, MacArthur still had a lot to learn about the importance of air power and the use of a navy. Marshall, however, was for the first time prepared to release major weapons to the Pacific as the American industrial machine had built up to the point where the Allies could afford to supply the Pacific Theater as well.

By this time it was clear that there were to be two major commanders in the Pacific operating from two different directions in the attack on Japan. Admiral Chester W Nimitz was unhappy about the prospect of placing naval forces under the command of Mac-Arthur, an army man, and therefore decided that he would launch his own

operation from Hawaii westward while MacArthur, as commander in the South-west Pacific, would push northward toward the same objective. This did not mean, of course, that MacArthur would have no substantial naval force under his command; but it did mean that Nimitz and MacArthur would be competing against each other to see who could defeat Japan quicker. Roosevelt, always fond of this confrontation tactic in labor relations, within his own government and in the political arena, approved of this scheme. The natural rivalry between the army and the navy could be used to the advantage of the Allies, who, after all, were interested in defeating Japan regardless of who got the credit. The navy hated MacArthur and the admirals welcomed this sort of confrontation. Stimson wrote that Mac-Arthur was 'a constant bone of contention,' and although his brilliance as a general was not always matched by his tact, 'the navy's bitterness against him

Above: The Japanese conquests and the Allied counteroffensive. MacArthur advanced through the East Indies and Nimitz across the Pacific.

seemed childish.'

In any event by July a policy toward victory in the Pacific was finally decided by the Joint Chiefs of Staff. It was announced that the objective was to seize the New Britain-New Ireland-New Guinea area. This directive of 2 July went on to say that a commander designated by Admiral Nimitz would take Santa Cruz, Tulagi (near Guadalcanal) and adjacent islands; MacArthur's forces would take the rest of the Solomons and the northeast coast of New Guinea, as well as Rabaul and adjacent positions in and around New Guinea and New Ireland. The island-hopping program had begun. MacArthur replied to this directive asking that the Tulagi-Santa Cruz operation be deferred in favor of the rest of the program, but Admiral King insisted on handling it according

Above: MacArthur explains his strategy for the liberation of New Guinea to Admiral Chester W Nimitz, who commanded Allied forces in the Central Pacific command areas.

to the directive. MacArthur was correct in his second thoughts about the operation; he did not have the means to do all of this, but after having received messages from MacArthur for so long that he wanted to press ahead, King could see no reason why MacArthur had changed his mind all of a sudden.

MacArthur, it is true, was now confronting the realities and difficulties of the task he had before him. But the persistent lack of confidence MacArthur had in Washington and the Joint Chiefs, a feeling which he did not pretend to disguise, was counterproductive. He continued to argue that a second front in Europe was not realistic and that the best way to relieve the pressure on Russia was to launch a sustained attack on Japan with most of America's forces. These remarks not only made the situation vis à vis Washington worse; they were politically naive in the extreme. Russia was not at war with Japan. What possible good would it do for Russia to have Japan defeated, except to eliminate

a former and perhaps future enemy? Russia and America, for that matter, were obsessed with defeating Germany. With Russian troops pushed back 1000 miles or more into their own territory by the Germans, with America's European Allies, with one or two exceptions, already occupied by Germany, this was not an altogether unreasonable position.

Nevertheless, MacArthur took positive steps to fortify New Guinea and prepared to attack Rabaul. The Japanese continued to press forward in New Guinea and Australian forces were slowly pushed back. On 25 August a second prong of the Japanese attack on Port Moresby began with a landing of some 2000 marines near Milne Bay airstrip. The Australians held back the advance after 10 days of intense fighting and then began to push them back. This was the first defeat of a Japanese amphibious force in the war. MacArthur was understandably concerned about the Milne Bay operation, as well as the fact that the attack plan had resulted only in the Allies' attempting to hold on to their forward bases. MacArthur was unfamiliar with the problems of fighting in the mountains of East Asia and did not visit New Guinea personally until Octo-

ber. His optimism was still his greatest enemy. Invariably he would have to revise his overestimation of Allied capabilities after having suffered setbacks. Part of the problem was that he was not fully informed. This was partly his own fault. His commanding, even forbidding, appearance which he actively cultivated made it difficult for him to have good working relationships with many of his subordinates. Major General George Brett, his air commander, came under heavy criticism from MacArthur, and Brett knew that he was not liked by MacArthur. Therefore Brett had only been able to see MacArthur eight times in four months. When Brett was replaced by General George C Kenney, Kenney made it a point to be in and out of MacArthur's office, and an affection grew between the men which was to aid the Allied cause. Kenney's breezy ebullience cheered up MacArthur, still depressed from the earlier defeat.

From the time Kenney came to MacArthur the General's relationship with his other subordinates softened somewhat, therefore establishing a closer contact which would permit him to be more in touch with current information and intelligence than he previously had been. Personal loyalty to MacArthur was the key variable: without it and without stating it often to the General, one was kept from the inner circle and one eventually faced MacArthur's wrath. The court-like amosphere so evident in Manila was sustained in Australia, albeit with some modifications.

The first phase of the Joint Chiefs' offensive began on 8 August when the 1st Marine Division had been put ashore at Tulagi and Guadalcanal; beginning the long war of attrition and island-hopping. Although the Americans lost a carrier and two others had been damaged, heavy casualties had been suffered by the Japanese and by September 20,000 Allied soldiers were ashore. At the same time MacArthur carefully launched an offensive against the Japanese in New Guinea. MacArthur pressed Nimitz for more materiel, and Nimitz told him that he could spare nothing more. MacArthur then used

Below: Wounded US soldiers return from the front to a field hospital near Hariko, New Guinea in November 1942, soon after the counteroffensive was launched.

this as an excuse for not throwing heavy land forces into New Guinea, MacArthur would have to make the best of what he had, and he did. MacArthur was dissatisfied with the way the Australians had been unable to completely dislodge the Japanese from Milne Bay and told both Marshall and Curtin that he intended to send in American troops as reinforcements because he considered them superior to the Australian soldiers. While all this controversy was going on behind the scenes, the Japanese had ordered a withdrawal, as they had run out of supplies and could not sustain their offensive.

Argument faded in the light of the Japanese decision as the Allied troops pushed forward. The campaign in New Guinea had failed thus far because MacArthur had laid greater emphasis on taking Guadalcanal than on clearing Papua. This was a correct decision. If the Solomons could be taken the Japanese in New Guinea would be cut off and could be defeated more easily. Once men and supplies had been slowly built up MacArthur was prepared to make an all-out offensive in New Guinea. On 1

October the orders were issued for an Allied advance along two lines of attack, while other forces cleared the Milne Bay area. But MacArthur still emphasized taking Guadalcanal above the New Guinea offensive. Both Roosevelt and MacArthur had misgivings about the delay in taking the island and MacArthur went so far as to suggest on 31 October that if things became worse on Guadalcanal he was prepared to withdraw from the Allied-held section of the north coast of Papua in order to reinforce Guadalcanal. But air drops to the men in the Owen Stanley Range worked, even though maneuvering through the mountains was extremely difficult. The pincer movement heading toward Buna was now beginning to achieve results by November, at the same time as the Japanese suffered heavy losses in their defense of Guadalcanal. The Allies were unaware that the Japanese supplies and men were exhausted and by now they were facing an outnumbered enemy force which was holding on in much the same way as the beleaguered Americans had held on for so long on Bataan and Corregidor.

The Buna beachhead on the north coast of Papua was not easy to take, much to MacArthur's concern. Two weeks of fighting in November and a four-pronged Allied offensive had been stopped dead. Malaria and dysentery affected the Americans and the Japanese defenses were tough to crack. Allied supplies were still not plentiful and since the emphasis was still on Guadalcanal, few supplies reached the Allied forces surrounding Buna. MacArthur was now under criticism, since his Americans had been unable to capture the fortress and he was convinced that they had shown cowardice in the face of the enemy on New Guinea. He decided to send General Robert Eichelberger out there to sort out the difficulty and told him before he left to take Buna 'or don't come back alive.' Eichelberger was appalled at the situation near Buna. The condition of the troops was terrible and he agreed with MacArthur that the men lacked 'inspired leadership.' He replaced the commander in charge, Harding, with Major General Waldron, but realized that without reinforcements it would be impossible to take Buna. A fresh Australian brigade was sent but it was not until 2 January 1943 that Buna was finally taken.

Even though MacArthur was incensed at Australian criticism of his own American troops, he knew that there was an element of truth in their criticisms. Knowing that he would receive no reinforcements until after Guadalcanal had been taken, he had already pressed the Australians to return more of their combat troops from the Middle East, which, understandably enough, was not done, since these troops were engaged at El Alamein at the time. Despite all these difficulties, however, the last Japanese stronghold near Buna was taken on 22 January. Of the estimated 20,000 Japanese soldiers who landed on New Guinea, about 13,000 were killed. Allied losses were also formidable. There were over 3000 Allied dead, and 28,000 more were suffering from malaria. The cost in lives was greater in Papua for the Allies than on Guadalcanal, where roughly 1600 American lives were lost. The clean-up campaign on Papua was difficult as well, although on 4 January it is now known that Japan made the decision to abandon both Papua and Guadalcanal. Kenney's supply aircraft prevented Japan from sending in further supplies to their beleaguered troops in southern New Guinea. The real variable which had changed was control of the sea and the air, which by the end of 1942 had passed into the hands of the Allies. The Southwest Pacific was open for reconquest, and MacArthur was right to have emphasized going on the offensive when his supplies had built up to the point of superiority over the weary Japanese.

MacArthur, however, despite the fact that he now knew he was winning, was still issuing communiqués which greatly exaggerated Allied gains. These were designed to encourage morale at home, but have distorted the historical record. Often the reports would indicate that Allied troops had captured such-and-such an area, and this would give Americans in the States the impression that the effort probably was largely if not wholly American. Many reporters were later surprised to discover an area in Australian hands when they expected that the area had been taken by the Americans. MacArthur's distrust of Washington may have been one of his motives for issuing distorted and sometimes false communiqués, but MacArthur's inordinate desire for publicity and praise was probably the chief reason. The American public became convinced that the turning of the tide in the Pacific, which actually took place at the Battle of Midway, in which MacArthur played no part, was because of MacArthur's stunning victories and his military genius. It would be futile to denigrate MacArthur as a general; as a military man, although he made mistakes, he had few equals, but he wanted more than victory: he wanted glory.

Through these communiqués as well as through his real achievements MacArthur had become a hero to the American public. Senator Vandenberg of Michigan suggested that he be nominated on the Republican ticket at the presidential elections to take place in

1944, a prospect which MacArthur would have dearly loved. A long-time student of the Civil War, MacArthur would have seen the parallel with Mc-Clellan, the Union general who did not get along with his President, and who ran against his former commander in chief in the elections of 1864. Roosevelt would have seen the parallel too: Mc-Clellan ran against President Lincoln.

All this is not to imply that MacArthur did not deserve what praise he did receive; after the battle in the Bismarck Sea MacArthur was awarded the Distinguished Service Medal for the third time from his President and the British gave him the Grand Cross of the Order of the Bath. MacArthur's first year as Allied Commander in Chief ended with decisive success in the three main areas of attack despite the frustrations of the early days: Milne Bay, central Papua and southern New Guinea. Although

Below: Grumman Wildcat which caught fire during a raid on Japanese positions on Guadalcanal is saved by Marines who douse the flames with chemicals and dirt after its return to Henderson Field.

Bottom: Marines trudge through the mud and swamp of the Bougainville jungle which had to be taken inch by inch from its tenacious Japanese defenders during the Solomons campaign.

Top: Bombers of the US Marines on a raid over Rabaul, a well-defended Japanese-held island in the Southwest Pacific.
Above: Rehearsing landing operations. The Attack Troop Transport USS *McCawley* in 1943.

MacArthur made the broad plans and the men did the fighting, as is usual, MacArthur took the credit, which did not entirely endear him to his troops but which had extraordinary success in building his reputation as a military genius in the United States.

By the spring of 1943 the tide of victory had decisively turned in favor of the Allies. Germany had been repelled at Stalingrad, the Allies had made their long march across the desert in North Africa after the victory at El Alamein and were preparing to clear North Africa in their attempt to invade Italy from the south. Soon Italy would have left the war.

In the Pacific the results did not appear as decisive as in Russia and the Mediterranean. Although the Japanese had abandoned Guadalcanal and were

on the run in New Guinea, MacArthur still felt that he had been denied the materiel which he required to follow up the Japanese retreat with solid victories. Many of his units were tired, although the Seventh Fleet and Admiral 'Bull' Halsey's naval forces as well as the 13th Air Force and Kenney's 5th Air Force had now become formidable weapons. MacArthur now realized that his decision to maintain a separate air arm was a mistake and admitted this to Kenney, who had done so well in coordinating combined ground and air offensives. All this did not alter the Allies' long-term plans to continue with the assumption that Hitler was the main enemy, and that MacArthur and his colleagues should conduct primarily a holding operation in the Pacific until the war had been conclusively won by the Allies in Europe. About 30 percent of America's fighting strength was in the Pacific, and General Marshall intended to keep it that way. However, Roosevelt did agree that if an invasion of France did not take place in 1943, he would send more supplies to

the Pacific. The planning was to take Rabaul, secure the Aleutians and advance on Truk and the Marianas via the Marshalls and the Gilberts. Operations in the Southwest Pacific would come last along with the China-Burma-India theater in the list of priorities. Furthermore, the American navy was determined to make the victory in the Pacific largely a navy affair based around the carrier task forces and their supports.

MacArthur thought it incredible that the navy should take so narrow a view and allow inter-service rivalry to determine the course of the war. Through the insistence of Admiral King, MacArthur's and Nimitz's commands remained separate, despite MacArthur's urging and Washington's realization of the fact that this was not the most practical scheme. MacArthur was not the only egotist in the American military hierarchy, and King was as determined as MacArthur was to gain most of the glory for himself and for the navy. The trouble was that King was not as good a publicist as MacArthur.

In order to sort out the confusion a meeting was called among representatives of the Southwest Pacific Command, South Pacific and Central Pacific Areas in mid-March 1943. MacArthur's representative, Sutherland, presented a plan code named *Elkton*. The estimates showed that between 79,000 and 94,000 Japanese still remained in northern New Guinea and the Solomons with 383 aircraft, four battleships, two aircraft carriers and four cruisers. Reinforcements could be sent to them. The *Elkton* plan proposed a five-stage program: seizure of airfields on the Huon Peninsula to support landings on New Britain; seizure of airfields on New Georgia; seizure of airfields on New Britain and Bougainville; capture of Kavieng, isolating Rabaul; and finally, capture of Rabaul. Halsey and MacArthur demanded five more divisions to accomplish this task, plus 45 more air groups as well as additional naval forces. Sutherland had to tell MacArthur almost upon arrival at the meeting that these would not be forthcoming. After interminable discussions it was decided to accept a plan similar to *Elkton*, but that the operations in the Solomons would be conducted by Halsey, under the general supervision of MacArthur. Halsey went to Brisbane to discuss *Elkton* with MacArthur. The two men impressed each other enormously. MacArthur reported, 'I liked him from the moment we met.' Halsey felt the same, and at the time persuaded MacArthur to attack New Georgia at once, and some of the requirements MacArthur called for were met.

Admiral King was anxious for action to get under way since there had been continuing operations in New Guinea. After the conference called *Trident* was held in Washington in May, it was decided that a two-pronged offensive be launched against Japan in the Pacific and that MacArthur would get seven more divisions which he needed to carry out *Elkton*. The Joint Chiefs told MacArthur that they wanted to open an offensive against the Marshalls and asked him for a timetable. He suggested that the Allies move on a south-to-north axis, moving through New Guinea to Mindanao. He was still obsessed with getting to the Philippines as quickly as possible. He told the Joint Chiefs that the withdrawal of two marine divisions out of his theater would make

Above: MacArthur wishes Lt Col J J Colson well on his next assignment to parachute in near Lae, New Guinea, behind Japanese lines in Sept 1943.

the capture of Rabaul impossible. Finally an agreement was reached whereby he would take the northeast New Guinea coast by 1 September and attack New Britain on 1 December or thereabouts. Marshall also tried to take two bomber groups away from MacArthur's command but was unsuccessful this time. One might well ask why MacArthur always seemed starved of troops and weapons, and the answer is simple enough: priorities. One could suggest a spiteful policy on the part of Marshall and King, but this cannot be supported by the evidence.

Once MacArthur was placed in Australia in charge of operations in the Southwest Pacific he also had to accept a less active part in the early stages of the war. Hawaii, after all, was closer to Japan and the object of the war was to defeat and eventually occupy Japan, not the Philippines. With the Pacific theater low in priority in comparison with the Mediterranean, the Atlantic and the North Sea, MacArthur stood low in the priority totem pole. However much noise emanated from his headquarters nothing could alter that. But MacArthur was driven, not only to prove

himself and to avenge Bataan, but to protect his men and supply them properly, which is the object and duty of any conscientious commander. It was not the fact that MacArthur pushed for more troops and equipment; it was the way he did it.

By the end of June the south end of New Georgia had been taken by Halsey's men, and for several months the struggle in the Solomons continued with heavy loss of life, equal at that point only to Buna and Guadalcanal. It was not until early October that the Solomons were secured, and fighters based there were operating over Bougainville, the next stepping-stone to Rabaul. Kenney's air force was building up gradually while, at the same time, the Japanese were resisting the army on New Guinea less and less as the Allies slowly pushed forward. MacArthur was surprised by being awarded the Air Medal for the airborne and parachute attack by the 503rd Parachute Regiment on Nadzab in New Guinea in September. The New Guinea campaign picked up steam and after Lae was taken on 11 September, MacArthur decided upon a plan of amphibious landings behind enemy lines which was to become the hallmark of his operations in the Pacific. An advance on Finschhafen was ordered, and it was taken on 2 October. It was proposed by Marshall that similar tactics should be

Above: American troops unload ammunition from landing craft at Rendova Island during the reconquest of the Solomon Islands under MacArthur's command.

used to isolate Rabaul, which MacArthur claimed was essential for his naval base to support further operations. As it turned out, Rabaul was not taken and was not nearly as necessary to MacArthur's plans as he had thought. But as the Allies advanced, new plans were being made.

In August MacArthur sent his outline plan, code named *Reno*, to take the Philippines. After he had taken Rabaul (its possession was assumed) he would move along western New Guinea and thence to Mindanao via the Celebes. He claimed he could not reach Mindanao before 1945, perhaps later. The joint planners in Washington, however, assumed that MacArthur would either take or neutralize Rabaul by 1 February 1944, and would get to Hollandia in Dutch New Guinea no later than 1 August of that year. They insisted that MacArthur bypass Rabaul, despite MacArthur's insistence that he had to take it. They also stressed the point that Nimitz's operations in the central Pacific would take priority over MacArthur's, and they pointed out that Nimitz would be closer to the Philippines when his forward movement reached Palau than Mac-

Arthur would be at around the same time. The overall plan was to take the Philippines in 1945 and 1946 along with Formosa, the Ryukyus and Malaya. Japan would not be invaded until 1947 and would not be conquered until 1948. At the *Quadrant* conference in Quebec in August 1943 the British questioned the wisdom of advancing toward Japan on two axes and suggested that MacArthur merely hold his gains while Nimitz made the main drive across the Central Pacific. This would allow more men and materiel to be requisitioned for the invasion of Europe in 1944. This time Marshall and King came to MacArthur's aid and insisted on carrying their plans forward as scheduled. However, *Quadrant* offered MacArthur no new troops for his forces and no coherent program.

At this point MacArthur offered the Joint Chiefs a revised *Reno* plan which proposed a compromise on Rabaul: it would first be bypassed but captured later on. Rabaul would be isolated by 1 February and after operations on New Guinea, Mindanao would be attacked in February 1945. Despite Sutherland's efforts on MacArthur's behalf in Washington, it was decided that no new forces could be spared for MacArthur's plan. As a matter of fact, it is interesting to note that the policy of attrition toward the Joint Chiefs which MacArthur was waging was, to some extent, working.

Thirteen American army divisions were now in the Pacific employed against Japan compared with the same number employed against Germany. Although 75 groups of the Army Air Force were in the European Theater of Operations as compared with 35 in the Pacific, the heavy concentration of naval power in the Pacific at this time more than offset this number.

Furthermore Halsey was moving faster than he had expected against increased Japanese resistance. As the bombing of Rabaul was stepped up by Kenney, New Zealanders occupied the Treasuries. MacArthur decided to place some of his forces across the Japanese line of withdrawal after Finschhafen fell and a landing was made at Saidor on 2 January 1944. By the time the Japanese retreat across northern New Guinea ended in March 1944 with the Japanese back at Wewak, only 54,000 remained of the Japanese army of 90,000 or so which began the fighting in September. MacArthur now could see the way clear to return to the Philippines, his dream and preoccupation since he left Corregidor, with control of the sea lanes and the air largely in his hands. Meanwhile, the central Pacific campaign was gathering momentum, with Tarawa and the Gilberts taken in November 1943, and Nimitz was ordered to make a full-scale carrier attack on Truk. Nimitz and MacArthur would race for the Philippines after all, and with Nimitz's operations having priority from Washington, MacArthur could not expect to get further major shipments of supplies and men until after April 1944, as Nimitz was expected to attack the western Marshalls after having taken Truk, or, failing that, to seize the Palaus. They would be the launching pad for an attack on the Philippines, by bypassing Truk.

This was not entirely to MacArthur's liking. If anyone was to take the Philippines it would be him. Conspiracy theories, as usual, abounded in MacArthur's headquarters. Various groups were blamed for MacArthur's relegation to a back seat in the drive across the Pacific. At one time perfidy in the State Department, another time the Joint Chiefs or Roosevelt himself: all were charged with collusion with one sinister group after another: British imperialists, Communists; it had to have been someone's fault. Many innuendos crept into the frequent press conferences given by MacArthur; stage settings in which MacArthur could give a virtuoso performance before the dazzled eyes of the world, claiming victory, lack of support from the States and the brilliance of his own generalship. Reporters often were not taken in by the spectacular one-man shows, but enough of the aura of infallibility permeated the atmosphere so that the story could be transmitted to the States. As a result, a calculated effort on MacArthur's part, combined with an absolutely sincere belief that unpatriotic forces were at work within the States which hoped to deny him his triumphs, created an atmosphere of public opinion highly favorable to MacArthur.

It cannot be forgotten that most American newspapers, especially those in the West and Midwest, were owned by arch-Republican interests who resented Roosevelt's treble (it was to be quadruple) victory over the Republicans in the presidential elections since 1932. Many of their reporters knew it to be good for their own interests on the newspapers if an inordinate amount of glory were heaped on the shoulders of a general with arch-Republican sympathies while, at the same time, denigrating the role of the Democratic Commander in Chief, implying that he could have done more to win the war and bring the boys home quicker. MacArthur was in touch with Republican interests in the States. His political campaign was aimed over the heads of those in Washington on the Joint Chiefs and in the State Department and the White House who were opposed to what MacArthur was doing for legitimate reasons of their own. Failing to succeed politically with his superiors, MacArthur hoped to succeed at the ultimate power base, the people. In any event Sutherland was sent to Pearl Harbor to confer with the representatives of the three Pacific command areas on MacArthur's behalf, at the end of January 1944.

The conference agreed that the Marianas were too far away from Japan to use the B-29 bombers effectively, and that therefore Japan would have to be attacked from bases in China. In this event Truk could be bypassed by Nimitz after all and the attack carried directly to the Palaus. MacArthur obviously was upset by this decision and urged the

Joint Chiefs in February that if he were given more forces (again the same tired, repetitive note appears) he could be in the Philippines by the end of the year. He again suggested a huge force to be concentrated along the New Guinea-Mindanao axis in order to push northward at a fairly rapid speed. By this time his plans were quite unrealistic. It would have been impossible for Admiral King to justify slowing down the already successful Central Pacific advance, even though MacArthur had achieved far more in his area. While Nimitz had repelled the Japanese advance on Hawaii and managed to seize islands on the perimeter of Japan's defensive arc, MacArthur had taken most of northern New Guinea, and successfully defended southern New Guinea, and had gone on to take the Solomons and had advanced to New Britain. It may have been possible that the Joint Chiefs had begun to believe a bit of MacArthur's propaganda themselves. However grandiose his claims may have been, MacArthur had done an excellent job so far; or at least since he left Bataan.

The Joint Chiefs and the conference at Pearl Harbor insisted that MacArthur carry on with the bombing of Rabaul and that the strongly defended enemy

Below: Two tense US Marines during a mopping-up campaign on Bougainville Island. They are wearing camouflaged dungaree blouses and their steel helmets are covered in cloth.

base of Kavieng be taken rather than bypassed as Halsey suggested. Kenney believed that Manus 'was the most important piece of real estate' in the area and if that could be taken, the whole of the Bismarck Sea would be in Allied hands. Tasting victory, MacArthur insisted that he accompany the force to Los Negros, on which Manus was located, and further destroyers were allocated to the area to protect his person and hasten victory. On 28 February MacArthur landed at Cape Cretin in the cruiser *Phoenix* determined to go with the reconnaissance force to Momote airstrip. The landing was a success, and MacArthur pinned the DSC on the first man to reach the beach. After a day on shore MacArthur returned to the *Phoenix*. Momote airfield and Manus were taken in the days afterward, but even the taking of this strategic point brought MacArthur into another interservice dispute over who was to use the base. Nimitz proposed that control of Manus be given over to Halsey under his direct supervision, a proposal which made MacArthur all the more angry since he supervised the taking of the base personally. Halsey was called on the carpet and in a heated session with MacArthur, was accused of having been part of a vicious conspiracy to tear away MacArthur's authority. The base stayed under MacArthur's control.

The seizure of Manus completed the isolation of Rabaul and made its capture

quite unnecessary. By this time (March 1944) Nimitz was facing a 50,000 strong Japanese army in the central Pacific and the Japanese force in the Palaus was strengthened as well. At the same time the Japanese fleet was reorganized so that it was primarily a carrier force. The Commander of the Combined Fleet, Admiral Koga, was directing operations from his Palau base now that Truk had been abandoned, but with all the heavy losses sustained since the Battle of the Coral Sea, the carriers' air crews were poorly trained and hardly a match for the increasingly adroit Americans. Their main line of defense was planned to be along a line from Timor to Sarmi, the Palaus and the Marianas, thus placing the forces in New Guinea outside the arc. MacArthur's policy of bypassing strong enemy bases was to have even greater effect under these circumstances. For example, if Rabaul had been taken it would have cost the Allies more than any campaign against the Japanese in the Pacific thus far, but by isolating it its 100,000 troops were cut off from use by Japan without costing the Allies more than thousands of bombs. Taking Rabaul would have postponed MacArthur's return to the Philippines by many months and he knew it. Therefore Halsey was given free rein to expand his envelopment concept. Longer strides would be made toward the Philippines. On 25 March MacArthur informed Marshall that he would jump straight to Hollandia, first town and capital of Dutch New Guinea, 200 miles west of Japan's big base at Wewak. He had already told Marshall that he intended to be in the Philippines by December, and he meant to keep to that, if only for his own sake.

On 8 March at a meeting of the Joint Chiefs in Washington Sutherland once again repeated MacArthur's concept of a single drive toward the Philippines on a south-north axis which had been rejected so many times before. MacArthur still had not really accepted the Allies' decision to attack on two fronts, but the upshot of the talks was that MacArthur was given the go-ahead to move to Hollandia, continue his isolation of Rabaul and to move toward Mindanao by November; music to MacArthur's ears. But Nimitz was told to take the southern Marianas by June and the Palaus by 15 September. Inter-service rivalry was again put to the advantage of

the Allies; if Nimitz and MacArthur competed with each other in terms of victories over the Japanese, the end of the war could only come that much sooner. Formosa was made Nimitz's ultimate objective; MacArthur was to go for Luzon.

With Rabaul isolated and the Japanese forces in New Guinea neutralized and on the run, MacArthur was confident that he could make his way toward the Philippines with his naval support and air superiority. By April Hollandia was taken at a cost of little

Below: MacArthur and Maj Gen Horace Fuller inspect crates of airplane engines rendered useless by naval pounding preceding the invasion of a beach near Hollandia, New Guinea.

over 600 men, bypassing the 50,000-strong force at Wewak. As the Allies made their successful landing in Normandy, which made certain that the war in Europe would soon come to an end, MacArthur seized Biak, in July Noemfoor fell, and in September, Morotai. All of New Guinea was now in Allied hands and MacArthur was island-hopping toward the Philippines, all at a cost of very few lives. At the same time Nimitz advanced to the Marianas and Palaus, closer to the Ryukyus than MacArthur's forces. The Ryukyus were the last stage in the island hopping which was to end with Japan itself. At an enormous cost in lives Saipan had been taken, and in July Guam was recaptured at a cost of almost 1500 American lives. The Palaus

Above: Admiral Thomas Kinkaid and MacArthur on the flag bridge of the cruiser *Phoenix* during the bombardment of Los Negros.

were also a costly victory for Nimitz. Thus, whereas in Europe the Allies had stressed the importance of a single united drive toward Germany under Eisenhower's leadership, this sort of plan was made impossible because of the mutual jealousy of the army and navy in the Pacific.

Despite heavy American losses at Bougainville, MacArthur's race to the Philippines seemed to have been won. Both Nimitz and MacArthur were asked if they could step up their timetable for victory, and each said that they could not unless they were given more power. The Joint Chiefs were determined to hasten the end of the war by taking Japan, and were not as concerned as Nimitz and MacArthur seemed to be which areas before Japan were to be taken first. MacArthur urged the Joint Chiefs that the idea of bypassing the whole of the Philippines in favor of a final thrust toward Japan was politically unwise. Marshall felt that 'personal and political considerations' should not interfere with the main task at hand. He was convinced that if Formosa and the Ryukyus were taken this would help the final liberation of the Philippines, although this would mean that, like

Rabaul, they would be taken at the end of the war. Looking at the situation coolly in the summer of 1944, it was not in fact necessary for the Allies to take the Philippines in order to win the war against Japan, just as it was not absolutely vital for China, the Dutch East Indies, Singapore, Indo-China or any other part of Southeast Asia to fall into Allied hands if the ultimate objective was the occupation and capitulation of Japan.

As had been argued so eloquently in Europe (by Stalin, among others), the way to defeat Germany was not to attack Italy, but it was to attack Germany as quickly and as directly as possible. So it was with respect to Japan. There was more at stake than victory, according to MacArthur. He did not want to break faith with his abandoned and imprisoned troops in the Philippines; he did not want to break faith with the Filipinos; to him, and to his sense of honor, once the Philippines had been recaptured he had played his part in the war. The capture of Japan itself would be a glorious epilogue to his odyssey. A conference had to be called to settle these differences, of which Roosevelt was more than aware, and Nimitz and MacArthur were invited to meet the Commander in Chief on 26 July in Pearl Harbor. The question was not if the war was to be won, but when and how.

4: THE WARRIOR RETURNS

MacArthur had already proposed several plans for his role in the conclusion of the war. He claimed that he could be in Mindanao by 25 October, Leyte on 15 November and with the help of six divisions, Luzon by April 1945. The controversy between the army and the navy required that these points be settled at once. Tojo had resigned on 18 July, and in Japan itself, although the military was still in control of the government, as it had been since late 1941, if not in many respects earlier, inter-service rivalry had divided the military to a much greater extent than it had done among the Americans in the Pacific. A plan was afoot in Japan to make a compromise peace with the intercession of Russia, which was still neutral in the Pacific war, but little came of it. As is usual in history, the conclusion of the war and the making of a peace is far more complex a problem than fighting it, and Roosevelt, on the threshold of victory in both Europe and Asia, was anxious to have a confrontation of all parties involved before the final push was made; because the final push would determine the nature of the peace.

MacArthur was not certain that President Roosevelt would attend the meeting in Hawaii, but he was 'reasonably certain that he would be there.' Since MacArthur was invited personally and had never attended any of the big staff conferences (and as he later remarked, never was invited again), he assumed that something important was to be decided. Neither Marshall nor Admiral King was there, however, and since Roosevelt had just been nominated for a fourth term by the Democratic Party, it was felt in some circles that Roosevelt merely wanted to underline his role as Commander in Chief for the forthcoming elections in November 1944. Despite these criticisms, there seems little doubt that a conference at that time was not merely a political exercise,

Left: MacArthur returns to the Philippines in the company of President Sergio Osmena and fellow officers at Leyte in October 1944.

and MacArthur felt the same. He came with no staff officers other than personal ADCs, and he was a bit surprised to see that Nimitz had come prepared with assistants, maps and all the paraphernalia which usually accompanies conferences on a high level. Nimitz was surprised himself that MacArthur had not come as well equipped as he was, and when the conference opened on 28 July MacArthur was asked by Nimitz if he had been told what the subject of the conference was to be about; MacArthur replied that he had not. MacArthur later reported that Nimitz 'seemed amazed and somewhat shocked.' MacArthur felt that he was going to have to 'go it alone.'

Nimitz first presented a plan, which MacArthur felt certain was really King's, of bypassing the Philippines, and that all American forces in the Southwest Pacific area were to be transferred to Nimitz's direct command, save two divisions. The advance was proposed to continue through the Central Pacific and the Allies would invade Formosa in early 1945. MacArthur again opposed this scheme both on military and political grounds. He argued that possession of the Philippines would prevent supplies from reaching Japan from the south and force her to an early capitulation because she would be starved of vital resources. He felt that frontal attacks on Iwo Jima and Okinawa would be unduly costly, as many of Nimitz's earlier triumphs had been, and that the Philippines, with its largely pro-Allied population, would be a better base from which to launch attacks on Japan than Formosa, with its largely hostile population. Roosevelt argued that a frontal attack on the Philippines would be even more costly. MacArthur argued that the United States had a moral obligation to free the Philippines as soon as possible. He argued that 'to bypass isolated islands was one thing, but to leave in your rear such a large enemy concentration as the Philippines involved serious and unnecessary risks.' MacArthur replied to Roosevelt's argument that the cost in

Above: MacArthur and an aide move past a light antiaircraft gun during an inspection tour of the Allied positions near Aitape in April 1944.

Below: MacArthur, Roosevelt and Nimitz during their famous meeting at Scholfield Barracks in July 1944. MacArthur argued strongly for more men and supplies.

Allied lives would be too dear by saying, 'Mr. President, my losses would not be heavy, any more than they have been in the past. The days of frontal attack should be over. Modern infantry weapons are too deadly, and frontal assault is only for mediocre commanders. Good commanders do not turn in heavy losses.' With this riposte out of the way, MacArthur went on to explain his plan, which would include a reconquest of the Dutch East Indies by the First Australian Army after the Philippines had been taken. Admiral Leahy accepted his ideas and in the end, so did Roosevelt,

who apparently, according to MacArthur, was 'physically just a shell of the man I had known. It was clearly evident that his days were numbered.'

Roosevelt later asked MacArthur what he thought of the forthcoming election when they were inspecting troops together. MacArthur guardedly answered that he knew nothing of the political situation at home and denied that he would accept the nomination as the Republican candidate for President, a denial which Roosevelt doubted. Roosevelt had been worried for some months that MacArthur might accept the blan-

dishments offered to him by some Republicans; MacArthur would have made a formidable candidate at that time; the war hero returned. When the Australian Prime Minister, Curtin, had told Roosevelt some time earlier that he was certain that MacArthur wanted to retain his command, Roosevelt was 'obviously delighted.' Curtin later told MacArthur that 'every night when he turned in, the President had been looking under the bed to make dead sure that you weren't there.' The meeting with Roosevelt created renewed confidence of both men in each other.

The issue about a Philippine invasion was not finally settled until the Joint Chiefs met in September and agreed with MacArthur's proposal to attack Leyte on 20 December. Halsey's planes had attacked Mindanao and the Visayas and had reported that the areas were 'wide open,' while reports trickling in from the Philippines indicated that there were no Japanese on Leyte. Nimitz put forward the proposal that since that was the case, Mindanao should be bypassed and Leyte be attacked at once. At this point MacArthur was on his way to Morotai, but Sutherland replied to Marshall's inquiry that the reports that there were no Japanese on Leyte were incorrect. MacArthur's contacts with the Philippines were excellent and better than Nimitz's or Washington's, since he was in touch with a guerrilla network operating in the archipelago. He was certain that at least 20,000 Japanese were on Leyte and that reinforcements could easily be deployed to the island. The Joint Chiefs decided that MacArthur should be lent escort carriers and other vessels from Nimitz's command for the assault on Leyte.

MacArthur's plan called for a commando battalion to assault the entrance to Leyte Gulf on 17 October, and that the first waves would go ashore on the 20th. Halsey's Third Fleet would provide naval protection and Kenney's air forces plus the Australian RAAF Command would give close support and air cover. The fact that about 174,000 troops were available for this operation made it the largest yet undertaken in the Pacific. MacArthur still had to retain large numbers of troops behind the lines as so many Japanese troops had been bypassed already that sufficient numbers of Allied forces had to be maintained for mopping up operations as well as for the defense of bases in Bougainville, New Britain and Australian New Guinea. In any event with British approval, as Churchill was beginning to take a greater interest in MacArthur and the Pacific war now that the European war was entering its final stages, further Australian and American reinforcements were sent to MacArthur's command. Finally MacArthur was getting all the support he needed. A newly-formed American Eighth Army under Eichelberger was sent to relieve Krueger's Sixth Army of the remaining tasks in New Guinea and Morotai. In mid-October Kenney's and Halsey's aircraft struck at Japanese airfields throughout Formosa and the Philippines. The Japanese were convinced that they had repelled Halsey's ships, when in fact they had not sunk even one. But reports to the contrary convinced Japan that it would be worth while to mobilize a huge naval force to defend the Philippines as well as a tired but still effective air force. MacArthur was convinced that this would be the decisive battle of the Pacific war, and accompanied the convoy of 700 ships bound for Leyte.

The attack came at dawn and after the first forces had landed, MacArthur waded ashore, followed by Sergio Osmena, who was now the President of the Philippines after Quezon had died in August. In a downpour of rain MacArthur broadcast his message to the Philippine people. He said, 'People of the Philippines: I have returned. By the grace of Almighty God, our forces stand again on Philippine soil – soil consecrated by the blood of our two peoples.' It was a moment that MacArthur had long anticipated. He went on to say that Sergio Osmena was by his side and that the government of the Philippines was now 'firmly reestablished on Philippine soil.' He urged all Filipinos to 'rally to me. Let the indomitable spirit of Bataan and Corregidor lead on. . . . In the name of your sacred dead, strike! Let no heart be faint. Let every arm be steeled. The guidance of Divine God points the way. Follow in His Name to the Holy Grail of righteous victory.' No matter what one may think of such prose today, MacArthur's words had an overwhelming impact on the Filipinos. MacArthur urged Roosevelt, in a note which he scribbled out on the beach, to grant the

Philippines independence straightaway after the successful liberation campaign and asked Roosevelt to attend the ceremony in person. He wrote the President that 'such a step will electrify the world and redound immeasurably to the credit and honor of the United States for a thousand years.'

The Japanese were unimpressed by MacArthur's words or by the achievements of his landing force. On the 17th they became aware that the Americans were about to land on Leyte and threw a huge fleet into the battle. Had it not been for Admiral Kurita hesitating to press forward after his ships had sunk four ships of Admiral Kinkaid's Seventh Fleet because of the heavy air attacks mounted by Halsey, the Allies might have suffered a stunning setback. As it was the Japanese squadrons did not reach Leyte Gulf, and the attack was successful. MacArthur once more pointed out that lack of coordination between the navy and the army could have caused a major disaster for the Allies.

Below: MacArthur, Generals Sutherland and Krueger soon after the Leyte landings. Already the material buildup is under way.

Above: *LSM*-311 accompanied by a wave of LSMs, approaches the beach near Leyte as a part of the huge force of landing craft which disembarked men, tanks and supplies throughout the region.

Each day MacArthur went ashore to supervise the operations and one story, told by Kenney, described how Mac-Arthur walked around wearing his field marshal's cap and smoking his ever-present corncob pipe. One soldier looked up and nudged his comrade and said, 'Hey, there's General MacArthur.' The other soldier never even bothered to look around and replied, 'Oh yeah? And I suppose he's got Eleanor Roosevelt along with him.' MacArthur made certain that a plan to try disloyal Filipinos who were captured as traitors was scotched and continued to supervise the takeover of Leyte, supported by Roosevelt. There were many impious comments put forward by some members of the forces who accompanied MacArthur to the Philippines. It was patently obvious that MacArthur was wringing the last ounce of public senti-ment out of his return. Many claimed that MacArthur was trying to take all the credit, striding ashore to the Philip-pine beach while the cameras furiously clicked away. It was even mentioned that MacArthur could only have topped his performance by walking on the water to shore rather than through it. Despite his theatrical and quite typical per-formance, who can doubt that after the long struggles in New Guinea and through the islands MacArthur did not deserve his moment of melodrama? He had saved untold lives by finally agreeing to bypass Mindanao in favor of Leyte, and his strategy had paid off now that he

Above: An oil depot is blown up near Leyte. The fire was caused by the continuous naval bombardment which softened up the beaches and jungles before the Allied assault went in.

had sufficient supplies to back his opera-tions. His advice to Roosevelt was good; the United States would have stunned world public opinion had independence been granted soon after the victory. But, although there is a chance that Roosevelt, who loved amateur theatricals as much as MacArthur, might have done it, his death intervened, and the fight to recapture the Philippines went on.

By early December slow progress was being made. A landing on the west coast of Leyte went off without the loss of a single life, but the Japanese under General Yamashita were not prepared to give up the island or the Philippines themselves without a dogged fight. The airfields at Dulag and Tacloban were attacked, but the Japanese were faced with eight divisions, by far the largest

force they had yet faced in the Pacific war. On 18 December MacArthur was promoted to the rank of General of the Army, a new rank equivalent to that of Field Marshal. Eisenhower, Arnold and Marshall also received it at almost the same time. A story, perhaps apocryphal, is told of how this title evolved. Initially the title of Field Marshal was conceived, but since the first appointment was to go to George C Marshall, Marshall sug-gested that the title of Field Marshal Marshall might be slightly ludicrous, and the substitute General of the Army was proposed and accepted.

The mopping-up operation on Leyte, taken over from the Sixth Army by the Eighth Army on 26 December, proved to be far more serious than had been originally conceived. Although only about 60–70,000 troops were engaged on the Japanese side, the Allies had put more than a quarter of a million men in the field. The Japanese lost an estimated 48,000 of their number, while only

still meeting with opposition from Washington in the person of Admiral King. King still felt that Luzon should be bypassed in favor of Japan itself. Halsey, on the other hand, favored bypassing Formosa in favor of Luzon. Nimitz, at least until late September, favored attacking Formosa rather than Luzon. Almost without exception the ranking army and navy leaders in the Pacific were opposed to the seizure of Formosa; MacArthur had argued that a landing on Formosa would be very tricky and if, as Nimitz proposed, this operation would be followed by a landing at Amoy on the Chinese mainland, the Allies

would be bogged down on the continent of China in much the same way as the Japanese had been since 1937. Although a Chinese invasion might have been supported by Claire Chennault's 14th Air Force in Chungking, this would have been peripheral, at best. By mid-September Leahy, Marshall and even the senior naval commanders all favored MacArthur's plan rather than Nimitz's; only King remained adamant. Mac-

Below: MacArthur reads out his proclamation of the liberation of the Philippines from the steps of the Philippine Congress in Manila in the company of Philippine President Osmena.

about 3500 Allied lives were lost. Although MacArthur praised these troops vociferously, the American troops tended to get bogged down. America could put troops ashore in hostile territory and maintain supplies to them better than almost any other nation in the world, but a mechanized army finds itself more at home in the territory of another mechanized state like, say, Germany. When faced with alien territory, they tended to depend on heavy aerial bombardment and let the big guns do the work for them. This resulted in a slow progress but with comparatively little loss of life. The American army, composed largely of conscripts, unlike the marines or navy, lacked the *elan* that characterized many Continental armies, and certainly the Japanese army. Their officers had to make up for this lack of *esprit de corps* through firepower and greatly superior numbers.

MacArthur was determined to land on Luzon as soon as possible, but was

Arthur had told the Joint Chiefs that he would be able to attack Luzon on 20 December, and on 3 October MacArthur received a directive to attack on that date. Nimitz, meanwhile, was told to attack Iwo Jima in January 1945 and Okinawa in March. The Joint Chiefs had decided, after all, to attack in the direction of Japan, their enemy, rather than China, their ally. MacArthur was relieved. He would not be cheated out of taking the whole of the Philippine archipelago, rather than just bits of it, as he once had feared.

MacArthur decided to land at Lingayen Gulf as the Japanese had done

Below: MacArthur inspects the wreckage of Japanese aircraft at Mabalacat Airfield on Luzon in January 1945. Japanese resistance was ferocious and consistent.

three years before. He also assumed that the Japanese would fight to the end, defending the Cagayan River and the Sierra Madre Mountains at the north of Luzon which MacArthur had virtually left undefended in late 1941. His eventual plan was to take a weakly defended Mindoro on 5 December and make his landing on Luzon on the 20th, but the heavy fighting on Leyte delayed the operations to 15 December and 9 January respectively. Two regiments went ashore unopposed on Mindoro on the 15th and air strips were soon put in operation, but damage was done by Kamikaze raids as well as night air attacks. By the time the Luzon invasion was to take place, however, there were three fighter and two medium bomber groups based on Mindoro. At the same time Filipino guerrillas were strengthen-

ing their operations on Luzon, and they had provided intelligence for the whole of the Philippine exercise thus far. On the basis of this information MacArthur strengthened his invasion force for Luzon. The plan was to invade at Lingayen Gulf, then push across two flanks so as to secure both banks of the Agno River, and then thrust southward toward Manila. Halsey and the Third Fleet would cover the invasion within range of both Formosa and Luzon. Kamikazes attacked the mine sweepers incessantly and two battleships and three cruisers were damaged by these suicide planes. The Third Fleet arrived off Luzon on 3 January, and MacArthur boarded the cruiser *Boise*. Submarines and Kamikazes continued their assaults and 11 more vessels were damaged. Several more ships were seriously damaged by these attacks in the days before the invasion but they had already run out of steam. Much of the Japanese air power had been destroyed in earlier raids and Kamikaze attacks, and Yamashita knew, just as MacArthur knew little more than three years before, that the loss of air superiority before an invasion took place spelled the success of the invasion. Yamashita planned to make his last stand in the northern mountains.

Above: US Army flame throwers advance on Clark Field, the largest air base in the Pacific, which the Japanese tried unsuccessfully to hold.

The landing on 9 January found MacArthur wading ashore after his troops as President Osmena announced on the radio to his people that MacArthur himself was on Luzon. There was little Japanese opposition to the landings, but the retreat was slow and tedious, with heavy loss of life on both sides. The fighting around Clark Field, the major air base in the islands, was especially fierce, and MacArthur followed his troops toward Manila. MacArthur was awarded his third Distinguished Service Cross. For MacArthur this was a moment of genuine emotion. The Philippines were his country as much as the United States. His father had served there at the climax of his career and MacArthur himself had spent much of his life in service there. It was on the Philippines that he had suffered his worst defeat, and he was worshipped by the Filipinos. General Kenney drop-

ped in one evening to report to him as the campaign progressed. MacArthur told him that he could not eat because of fatigue. The next morning before daybreak Kenney asked the orderly to say good-bye to MacArthur because he was leaving early. The officer told him that MacArthur left for the front over two hours before. Kenney is reported to have said, 'The guy must be nuts. If he works overtime, he'll lose his union card.' MacArthur's enthusiasm was only matched by the response of the Filipinos. The guerrillas sprang into action upon hearing of the landings in Luzon and made life increasingly difficult for the retreating Japanese.

As the Americans advanced MacArthur made his way to the concentration camps where belligerents and civilians alike who were left in the islands were taken for the duration of the war by the Japanese. He was greeted by ragged, half-starved GIs at the Santo Tomas camp who wept and tried catching his hand. They wept at the sight of him. MacArthur was moved to near-speechlessness. The Americans entered

Manila on 3 February, almost four weeks after their landing, half as fast as the Japanese when they took the city in 1942. The enemy fought on sporadically for two more weeks before the city was firmly in American hands. In Manila, as elsewhere, Filipinos pressed round him, trying to touch him or kiss his hand and regale him with tears and thanks. His triumph was overwhelming. MacArthur was with his men and went to his penthouse atop the Manila Hotel where he had made his headquarters before the war. He had heard that everything was intact, untouched. As he approached the hotel, the Japanese set fire to it. He watched as his library of military history and the personal belongings of a lifetime, which had withstood the whole war, went up in flames.

By the end of January the XIV Corps had secured Clark Field and were on the road leading to Bataan. On the 29th XI Corps, led by Major General Charles P Hall, landed three regiments at the head of Subic Bay, the major naval base on Luzon. This operation would seal off the Bataan Peninsula while at the same time preventing the Japanese from landing any troops from Formosa to surprise the Americans in Lingayen Gulf. To secure the southern approaches to Manila, MacArthur sent Eichelberger to land one parachute regiment south of the city, and when the drop took place on 3 February, it was unopposed. Meanwhile, the fight to eradicate the last remnants of Japanese resistance in Manila continued. Eventually the remaining opposition was trapped in the Intramuros, the old walled city section of Manila. After over a week of heavy artillery bombardment the infantry moved in on 23 February, but the last diehards did not capitulate until 3 March. Heavy casualties were inflicted on both sides before the smoke cleared. MacArthur insisted that no delay should prevent the reestablishment of the powers of the Philippine government even while the fighting for Manila continued. Although the city was rapidly being reduced to a smoldering ruin and the centuries-old Intramuros levelled, MacArthur restored constitutional government to the Philippines at a ceremony at the Malacanan Palace, sometimes known as the Philippine White House. The ceremony, held on 27 February, was a solemn one.

Left: MacArthur observes the shelling of Japanese positions from an artillery post in Fort Stotsenburg on Luzon in late January 1945. US artillery played a vital part in subduing Japanese resistance.

Below: MacArthur examines a map in a jeep near Camling, Luzon, 20 January 1945. This is one of the first photographs showing him wearing five-star insignia on his shirt collar.

Above: MacArthur meets Admiral Lord Louis Mountbatten, Supreme Allied Commander of the Southeast Asia Theater, during his stopover in Luzon in July 1945.

Right: Philippine and US GIs on a search and destroy mission in Fort Stotsenburg, Luzon which is at the southwestern tip of Clark Airfield during the heavy fighting to recapture this key strong point.

Below: MacArthur, second from the left, strolls down the main street in Dagupan, Luzon after the capture of the town in February 1945 by the American forces.

MacArthur later described his trip to the Palace through the once-tree-lined streets past the rubble and the unburied dead. When he finally arrived at the Malacanan, he found it untouched, with its stained glass windows, crystal chandeliers and tapestries all in place. In the presence of President Osmena, his senior commanders, and Osmena's cabinet he thought of all the memories he had of Manila, where he had courted his second wife, where his son had been born, where his father had served, and all the struggles and hopes that he had lived with in the Philippine capital. As he spoke to a hushed audience he recounted how his forces had fought back to regain Manila and the Philippines at such an exorbitant cost. His voice broke and he was unable to go on as emotion overcame him.

MacArthur had insisted that the same degree of independence as formerly should be restored to the Philippine government pending a final decision from Washington. It was expected that full independence would be granted very soon, although it was not done until 4 July 1946. Meanwhile the XI Corps had cleared Bataan, an operation which MacArthur personally supervised. Under heavy bombardment for weeks, the fortress island of Corregidor fell to the Americans, after having been defended almost to the last man by 5000 Japanese troops. Most of them died on the island; only 26 were taken prisoner. MacArthur visited the island on 2 March in four PT boats, the same number which left with his party when he embarked for Australia in 1942. Many of the same men who were with him that day returned with him to Corregidor to inspect the old headquarters. He raised the American flag atop the old flagpole.

By this time all of the main strategic objectives on Luzon had been taken. Although there were still Japanese forces, the task remained to wipe out Yamashita's troops still in the northern highlands of Luzon. MacArthur was determined to eradicate every vestige of Japanese power in the Philippines, and even hoped to do the same in the Dutch East Indies, which he wanted to clear. Washington rejected this last proposal, and in so doing permitted Sukarno's Indonesian independence movement to seize power after the capitulation of Japan, since, aside from Dutch New

Above: The remains of Manila. By February 1945 Manila, thanks to bombing and house-to-house fighting, suffered more damage than any city in Asia outside the Japanese Home Islands.

Below: Allied troops march past the ruins of the Post Office building in Manila during the capture of the centuries-old Intramuros section of the city. The Japanese were led by Adm Iwabuchi.

Guinea, there were no Allied troops occupying the Dutch East Indies when Japan finally fell. By April the sea route through the Visayas was cleared, and by the end of June the Japanese only held about a 25 mile square area, near the summer capital of Baguio. The Americans lost 8500 lives in securing Luzon and upon capitulation there were still some 50,000 Japanese troops who had held out, almost 40,000 of these being with Yamashita's group. Baguio fell on 26 April, but the Japanese retreated to a small pocket northeast of the city. During this same period Iwo Jima had been taken with a heavy loss of American lives. The Japanese defense of the Philippines had been admirable. They engaged tens of thousands of American troops, just as the Japanese had stalled American naval and air forces at Iwo Jima, and by late spring, 1945, after

Below: MacArthur makes an inspection tour on his return to Corregidor, scene of his most bitter defeat in 1942. There was little left of the island after two invasions.

Germany had capitulated, the Allies were still far from achieving complete victory over Japan. It was widely felt that the war in the Pacific would last quite a long time yet, and that Japan would have to be fought over for a year to a year and a half before its spirit would be broken. The Kamikaze missions, which grew in ferocity during the first months of 1945, convinced MacArthur and most other American military leaders that Japan would not go down without a long and arduous fight on the four main islands themselves after the Ryukyus were occupied.

On the day MacArthur's troops entered Manila a conference took place on the other side of the world which was to influence the course of the war in the Pacific. Yalta, the penultimate Allied conference, attended by Roosevelt, Churchill and Stalin, decided that the USSR would enter the Pacific war two to three months after the capitulation of Germany. Russia was promised southern Sakhalin, Port Arthur and

Dairen in southern Manchuria, which they had lost to Japan in 1905 as well as an occupation zone in Korea, their old sphere of influence, and the Kurile Islands. Roosevelt's reasoning was based on reports that he had received from the Far East, including reports sent by MacArthur. Japan would be a hard nut to crack, and with their reputedly large reserve force still untested in the Kwantung Peninsula, the Allies felt that Russian help would bring the war to a speedier conclusion. Although it is now known that the Kwantung Army had been greatly reduced and was not nearly the formidable weapon it was thought to be, it was not unreasonable to ask the USSR to help win the war in the Pacific, despite the fact that this decision was to come under heavy criticism later, with MacArthur one of the chief critics. The fight on Okinawa, which began on 1 April, did not lead the Americans and their allies to change their point of view, as the Japanese fought bitterly against increasingly powerful opposition.

Left: Stalin, Roosevelt and Churchill at their summit conference in Teheran in Nov 1943, when Stalin first offered to bring the USSR into the Pacific war.

On 1 May, MacArthur's Australians opened the first phase of what was to be a longterm plan to recapture the Dutch East Indies. Roosevelt had not wanted MacArthur to engage American troops in these operations and MacArthur, distrustful of the British, was unhappy about the prospect of sending British forces to clear the Indies, as he felt that if they took the territory, it would be difficult to dislodge them. Although the problems of Raffles in Java during and after the Napoleonic Wars were an

Below: MacArthur is greeted by internees at the prison camp at Santo Tomas University on Luzon. Horror stories from these camps shocked the American public.

example of what could have happened, it is doubtful whether MacArthur's fears had any real basis. The British had an alliance with the Netherlands and had promised them – or at least Churchill had done – that the Indies would be restored to Holland after the war.

Roosevelt died on 12 April, and was replaced by Harry S Truman, former US Senator from Missouri and Vice-President since January 1945. Although MacArthur had a grudging respect for his onetime nemesis, Roosevelt, he knew little about Truman and felt that he knew a good deal more about the situation in the Far East than his new Commander in Chief. In any event, Mac-Arthur felt that if Australian (they were

near enough to be British in his eyes) forces moved into the Dutch East Indies under his own command, they could be prevented from repeating Raffles' errors in trying to remain in possession of the archipelago. They were assigned to seize Tarakan near eastern Borneo as the first step in this operation. MacArthur refused to use British troops under Mountbatten's command for the recapture of the Indies for another reason: they would be cutting into what MacArthur felt was his territory and reap the fruits of victory which they had done so little to merit, at least with respect to the Indies. Their record in Burma speaks for itself. Furthermore, the oil of Borneo could be used to supply MacArthur's own campaigns.

General Sir Thomas Blamey of the Australian army strongly objected to MacArthur's implication that the Australians were not to be trusted. He wanted to have effective control over his own forces and complained bitterly

to the Australian Defense Department. When Blamey met MacArthur they compromised by agreeing that although the Australian I Corps would operate under Blamey's effective control, with the 'administrative functions' performed by Blamey's advance HQ at Morotai, the unit would remain under MacArthur's general command. Blamey had no intention of withdrawing Australian troops from Australian New Guinea – there were still some Japanese soldiers left withering on the vine behind Allied lines who were maintaining a rear-guard action – for combat in the Dutch East Indies until the last remnants of Japanese resistance were rooted out. In this respect Blamey, quite naturally, looked upon Australian New Guinea in much the same way as MacArthur viewed the Philippines. It was a matter of his country's honor, its self respect.

Plans for Borneo were finally sorted out by the Combined Chiefs of Staff. The plans were revised to assure that Tarakan would be taken in May, Brunei Bay in June and Balikpapan in July. The British, contrary to what MacArthur thought about them, were not really anxious that action be taken against Borneo. Japan, after all, was the principal objective and Borneo was in the opposite direction from Japan with the bulk of Allied strength now in the Philippines. The British point of view did not prevail, and it seems ironic that in the effort (ostensibly) to prevent British imperialist interests from reasserting themselves in Southeast Asia, MacArthur made every effort to replace their imperial designs by American ones, despite all he later said to the contrary.

MacArthur ruefully pointed out in his memoirs that the restoration of Dutch rule to the Indies would have provided a more orderly administration of the area, and that the plans he harbored for a complete reconquest of the Indies were foiled by maladministration from Washington, the result of which was the 'chaos' which ensued after the Japanese capitulation. This chaos, one is to assume, took the form of the establishment of the Indonesian government under Sukarno and its declaration of independence on 17 August 1945. That there was political and military strife in Indonesia after the end of the war cannot be doubted, but MacArthur can hardly claim to be an anti-

Above: MacArthur visits Bilibid Prison in Manila where combatants were held as POWs throughout the war. Nearby Santo Tomas University was the civilian internment camp.

imperialist when he sought so hard to reestablish Dutch, in favor of British, imperial interests in Southeast Asia after the war.

An Australian brigade group landed on Tarakan on 1 May. Soon afterward Germany capitulated and the Australian government, at Blamey's request, asked MacArthur if he could reconsider his plan to continue to Balikpapan rather than sending Australian forces along with the Americans against Japan. The Australian people were as anxious as the other allies to end the war in the Pacific as soon as possible now that the fighting in Europe was over. MacArthur insisted that the operation in Borneo be continued and that the Australians continue to make their way toward Balikpapan, and they agreed despite their misgivings. MacArthur even went so far as to go ashore with the Australian forces when they secured Brunei Bay in June, and did the same thing at Balikpapan on 1 July when an amphibious attack was launched there involving 33,000 troops. It was to be the last operation of MacArthur's Southwest Pacific Command and it was done expertly, as usual.

Within three weeks it was all over except for some mopping-up activity.

By July 1945 the fight on Luzon was still not over. It was the largest land campaign of the Pacific war and involved 15 American divisions as well as substantial numbers of Philippine troops, more than the Allies had in Sicily, or Burma, or Okinawa. MacArthur's insistence that the last remnants of Japanese opposition be eradicated on the Philippines before committing his troops to the invasion of Japan did not shorten the war in the Pacific. His plans, had they been carried out, to recapture the Dutch East Indies would not have made the war any shorter either. His original scheme of island hopping and bypassing the Japanese whenever possible, which was so successful on New Guinea and after, should have been continued, but MacArthur's conception of his own honor and his nation's stood in the way. However, MacArthur was still under the impression that the war in the Pacific was far from over, and had told President Truman that he would need at least another year, probably more, to defeat Japan on her own ground.

It was on the basis of this and other similar arguments that Truman made the decision which was to end the war so dramatically – the dropping of the atomic bomb on Hiroshima. MacArthur had no prior knowledge of this.

The seizure of Okinawa made the bombing and subsequent invasion of

Japan possible by July 1945. The fire raids on Japanese cities, particularly Tokyo, advocated by Major General Curtis LeMay, were having a devastating effect on the civilian population, but the Japanese were thoroughly prepared to fight to the bitter end.

MacArthur and Nimitz had already made preliminary plans for the invasion of the home islands, which was to take place on Kyushu, Japan's southernmost island, and was to be of unparalleled magnitude. Although Nimitz and MacArthur would cooperate, the divided command was to be sustained even at this terminal stage. The Allies expected a force of approximately 2,000,000 men to greet them in Japan itself, and it was thought that an initial landing force of about 10 divisions with a reserve of three more would be required. A landing near Tokyo was to follow, and 14 more divisions plus about 11 more in reserve would be required. On 17 July the final wartime conference began at Potsdam, outside occupied Berlin, in which Truman, Stalin and Churchill met to discuss the Allied settlement in Europe as well as the concluding stages of the war against Japan. Churchill was soon replaced by Clement Attlee, whose Labour Party was elected to office at the British general elections which took effect while the conference was in session.

As the conference began Truman was informed of the successful atomic tests then under way in New Mexico, and soon after authorized the dropping of this weapon on Japan in an attempt to avoid the necessity of an Allied invasion which was sure to cost tens of thousands of American lives. The Japanese were offered the choice of facing the new weapon, described to them in the broadest terms, or capitulating at once. Japan characteristically refused to accept defeat on the basis of threats and refused to negotiate a surrender which the Allies had made clear years before would be unconditional. On 6 August 1945 a single American airplane, the *Enola Gay*, dropped the most devastating weapon yet known to man on the city of Hiroshima and uniformly levelled the city.

President Truman announced this event to the American people some hours later, telling his countrymen that the atomic bomb had more power than 20,000 tons of TNT. He went on to point out that the Americans were determined

Above: MacArthur watches from a balcony of Manila's City Hall in August 1945 with fellow soldiers as the Japanese delegation arrives to make their formal surrender.

to continue these attacks in order to 'completely destroy Japan's power to make war.' On 8 August, the USSR, ironically keeping to its word given at the Yalta Conference that it would enter the war two or three months after the capitulation of Germany, attacked Japanese forces in Manchukuo, Japanese-controlled Manchuria, three months to the day after the war in Europe ended. The Soviet Union formally declared war against Japan. The Japanese government refused to accept defeat even after the first bomb was dropped, so on the following day, 9 August, a second atomic

bomb was dropped on Nagasaki. By 10 August Japan had had enough. On 12 August Truman ordered his air force to cease its incessant bombing raids on Japan. On 15 August Japan surrendered.

Although MacArthur did not participate in the negotiations which led to the capitulation, on the day Japan surrendered MacArthur was appointed Supreme Commander Allied Powers, which placed him in charge of organizing the ceremonies of surrender as well as the occupation and reorganization of postwar Japan. He directed the Imperial government to send a delegation to Manila to receive their instructions concerning the surrender ceremonies. Sutherland handled most of the talks with the Japanese, who were extremely cooperative except for one point: they

about how the Japanese would treat their conqueror, inasmuch as there were still 22 Japanese divisions, comprising over 300,000 men, on the Kanto Plain near Tokyo and Yokohama. However the broadcast of the Emperor, an unprecedented act, tended to calm most of the population. Repeating the words of his predecessor, the Emperor Meiji, who had remarked that Japan had to 'accept the unacceptable, endure the unendurable' when the Far Eastern Triplice had thwarted Japan's attempts to take over Port Arthur, Dairen and the Kwantung Peninsula after the Sino-Japanese War in 1895, the Showa Emperor, Hirohito, told his stunned nation that 'as he [Meiji] endured the unendurable, so shall I, and so must you.' Hirohito waited in the Imperial Palace not knowing what his fate was to be. MacArthur was determined from the outset that the divinity of the Emperor should be destroyed, but he also had sufficient knowledge of the Japanese people to know that to eliminate the Emperor himself would be a serious error.

The Potsdam Declaration of a month before was to be the basis of MacArthur's new position in Japan, and it was a broad enough brief to suit MacArthur's attitude. It stated that those who brought Japan to war should be eliminated 'for all time,' that Japan should be occupied

Below: Philippine President Sergio Osmena is congratulated by MacArthur in the General's office in Manila's City Hall on the day of the Japanese surrender.

militarily, that stern justice should be meted out to 'war criminals,' and that democratic government and the freedoms which usually accompany it should be established in Japan; the Allies would withdraw their occupation forces once this mission had been completed. On 29 August MacArthur received a summary of the US Initial Post-Surrender Policy for Japan which had been prepared by the State Department as well as the War and Navy Departments. This document gave MacArthur the authority to control Japan 'through Japanese governmental machinery and agencies, including the Emperor.' Therefore it had been accepted that the Emperor would remain on his throne, although the character of his regime would change radically. MacArthur's initial conception that the Emperor should be retained as an instrument of peace was maintained by the American government, and MacArthur was to have free rein in Japan based on the broad proposals outlined in the document.

From 25 August on aircraft and a few infantry were landed in Japan under Eichelberger, and their fears that they would meet severe diehard opposition proved unfounded. The Emperor's speech had shattered the will of the Japanese people to continue their struggles. Veneration, far stronger than mere respect, for the Emperor was so great that it was unthinkable for most Japanese to oppose what he had said was his will. The voice of the Emperor had never been heard in Japan; he had

protested against the preparations at Atsugi airfield near Yokohama, which they felt could not be made ready in time for MacArthur's arrival. Propellers on all Japanese aircraft were ordered to be removed before he arrived, armed troops were to be withdrawn from the Tokyo area, and vehicles were to be provided for the use of the Allies. MacArthur would make his headquarters in the New Grand Hotel in Yokohama. Many of MacArthur's advisers advised him not to go to Atsugi, which had been used by Kamikaze pilots who denounced the surrender in no uncertain terms, even dropping leaflets to the Japanese people and threatening to bomb the battleship *Missouri* on which the formal surrender ceremonies would take place. There was a great deal of uncertainty

Above: GIs from the 32nd Infantry Division watch the Kay Kyser USO show in the rain on Luzon in late 1945. Such shows helped to maintain morale and were much appreciated.

never made broadcasts as Roosevelt, de Gaulle and King George had done. His position in the Japanese social and governmental hierarchy could not be challenged. The war had been fought in his name. He was, more than any Western monarch had ever been in the heyday of absolute monarchy, the fountainhead of government and power. Therefore, when he surrendered publicly and accepted public humiliation at the end of the war, the vast majority of the people of Japan followed him. It was, indeed, only through him that any opposition to the Allied occupation which did exist could be suppressed. The Japanese, whose islands had never been occupied by an invader in all their long history, awaited their fate.

At the same time more than 350 ships of the American and British Pacific Fleets steamed toward Tokyo Bay. Even the locale of the surrender ceremonies was contested by inter-service rivalry, which continued to the very end. A

compromise was reached when it was agreed that MacArthur of the army would accept the surrender on Nimitz's flagship the *Missouri,* which also pleased Truman, whose home state was Missouri. A regiment of Marines would be sent ashore while army troops landed at Atsugi. Furthermore, the army and navy would share in the initial occupation of Japan. The Eighth Army and Third Fleet were responsible for Honshu, the principal island of Japan, from Kobe eastward. The Sixth Army and Fifth Fleet were to occupy western Honshu, Kyushu and Shikoku, the North Pacific Fleet was to occupy Hokkaido, and the Seventh Fleet and XXIV Corps were to occupy Korea south of the 38th Parallel. Russia was to occupy (and was rapidly occupying) Manchuria and Korea north of the 38th Parallel. Ships of the Third Fleet entered Tokyo Bay on the 28th and troops were landed at Yokusaka on the 30th.

Early in the morning of the 30th MacArthur boarded his aircraft *Bataan* for the seven-hour flight to Tokyo. MacArthur made notes on the plane which were to become the broad outlines for his policy as military governor

for the next six years. At 1400 the *Bataan* circled Atsugi airfield and landed, giving MacArthur a view of Mount Fujiyama as the aircraft turned. MacArthur quietly got out of the plane, dressed in an open-necked shirt and puffing on his corncob pipe. Despite the fact that there was great apprehension that at the last minute diehard Japanese would storm the small military contingent which was there to greet him, MacArthur appeared calm and resolute. General Eichelberger greeted him and as they shook hands MacArthur said: 'Bob, from Melbourne to Tokyo is a long way, but this seems to be the end of the road.' Along the road to Yokohama a long line of Japanese soldiers guarded the route, giving MacArthur the same respect that they paid the Emperor; their backs were turned as his cortege passed. Yokohama seemed like a ghost town when MacArthur arrived. Shop windows were boarded up, blinds were drawn and the sidewalks seemed deserted. He went to the New Grand Hotel, where he planned to stay until he made his formal entry into Tokyo. There was no incident whatever, and the hotel management treated him with servile deference. After checking into his suite, MacArthur simply repaired to the dining room where he devoured a steak dinner.

As prisoners from POW camps were being released MacArthur insisted that Generals Wainwright and Percival be brought to Japan to attend the ceremonies on the *Missouri*. On the night of the 31st they arrived at MacArthur's hotel, haggard, drawn and emaciated from their years in prison camp. MacArthur was just sitting down to dinner when he heard that they had arrived. As MacArthur rose to greet them in the lobby, the doors of the dining room swung open and there was Wainwright. MacArthur later reported that 'his uniform hung in folds on his fleshless form. He walked with difficulty and with the help of a cane. His eyes were sunken and there were pits in his cheeks.' MacArthur embraced his colleague, who said he felt that he had disgraced MacArthur and his nation by capitulating at Corregidor. MacArthur was shocked by this remark and said, 'your old corps is yours when you want it.' Wainwright was greatly relieved and MacArthur was moved beyond words.

The ceremony on the *Missouri* took place on 2 September 1945. The Foreign Minister of Japan, Shigemitsu, accepted the onerous duty of signing the surrender documents on behalf of the Emperor, and the Emperor had to personally persuade the second delegate, General Umezu, to agree to attend. The destroyers carrying the party to the *Missouri* arrived on that perfect day with blue skies and the American flag, the one used by Commodore Perry at Tokyo Bay almost a hundred years before, waving proudly in the breeze. Umezu was dressed in the olive drab of a general officer, with shiny cavalry boots and a ceremonial sword at his side. Shigemitsu Mamoru was dressed in a formal top hat, morning coat and striped trousers. Admiral 'Bull' Halsey, whose own ship was being used, was the host and greeted the Japanese delegation. There were row upon row of glittering uniforms of the representatives of all the Allied powers to greet the Japanese as well. The ship was jammed with military personnel, cameramen and reporters. MacArthur, in contrast with everyone, was wearing a simple uniform with his shirt open at the neck, without

decorations, his ubiquitous cap atop his head. Some Japanese thought his informal attire to have been a studied insult. More likely it was MacArthur's taste for the theatrical, so that he could stand out against all the sparkle and pomp of the uniforms surrounding him.

At precisely 0900 hours MacArthur strode out on deck and read from a bit of white paper that he held in his hand, standing behind a table which faced the Japanese. His speech was short. He said that the representatives of the Allied powers had come to restore peace with Japan. He added that it was not their purpose to meet 'in a spirit of distrust, malice or hatred. But rather it is for us, both victors and vanquished, to rise to that higher dignity which alone befits the sacred purposes we are about to serve. . . . It is my earnest hope and

Below: Col Paul Tibbets, whose B-29, *Enola Gay*, bombed Hiroshima on 6 August 1945, helping to bring the war in the Pacific to a rapid end.

indeed the hope of all mankind that from this solemn occasion a better world shall emerge out of the blood and carnage of the past – a world founded upon faith and understanding – a world dedicated to the dignity of man and the fulfillment of his most cherished wish – for freedom, tolerance and justice.' After the speech was over the Japanese delegates moved to the table to sign the surrender documents. At 0908 MacArthur put his name to the surrender, followed by representatives of the Allied powers. Shigemitsu nervously signed the document, slumping forward on the table, and Sutherland showed him where to sign. Wainwright and Nimitz were among those who signed for the United States. When the representatives of the other nations (China, the United Kingdom, the Soviet Union, Australia, Canada, France, the Netherlands and New Zealand) had signed, MacArthur announced: 'Let us pray that peace be now restored to the world and that God will preserve it always. These proceedings are closed.' A deafening roar from over a thousand planes which flew past overhead brought the historic ceremonies to a close. Soon afterward MacArthur broadcast to the American people. World War II at last was over.

In 1945 MacArthur reached the pinnacle of a long and honored career. He was a great soldier. His strong and dominating character was strengthened by his experiences in World War I, where he displayed courage and leadership matched by very few indeed. But a warrior in peacetime undergoes subtle changes of character. The years between the wars were frustrating ones for MacArthur, even though his career in these years was marked with distinction. MacArthur craved action and he also recognized the need for the United States to wake up from its postwar lethargy and irresponsibility to the realities which the 1930s presented – a renascent Germany, an aggressive Italy and an increasingly belligerent Japan. Deprived of the funds necessary to build up the defenses in the Philippines, his petulant attitude prevented him from doing more than what was done. He blamed Washington for his failings, and up until the time of his second marriage, his pride got the better of his judgment. The court-like atmosphere in Manila which appealed to his fantasies of grandeur and melodrama caused a deterioration in his character that was to have shattering consequences when the war broke out. Regardless of what he may have said to the contrary, MacArthur had not done an adequate job in preparing the Philippines for the attack, and the fault cannot be laid at the feet of Washington exclusively. His retreat to Bataan and Corregidor was badly handled, and the poor morale among the troops there was largely his own fault.

It is difficult to guess what another man's thoughts are, and memoirs often serve as a disguise rather than a mirror to them. But one can hazard an assumption that in the first bleak months in Australia, MacArthur knew that he had failed. It was not so much out of revenge against Japan but as a sop to his own bad conscience that MacArthur pressed for an early return to the Philippines and, once there, insisted on driving every single Japanese soldier from the islands rather than concentrating on a major push toward Japan. His conduct of the

Below: Soviet naval flags are raised above Port Arthur after its capture from the Japanese after the war was over. At the same time Soviet forces penetrated into Korea.

Above: The ruins of Tokyo at the time of the surrender. The Japanese capital was reduced to rubble, as most of the buildings were made of wood and paper.

New Guinea campaign and his reconquest of the Philippines were brilliantly executed. Although detractors of Mac-Arthur have argued that it was Halsey as much as the Joint Chiefs who engineered these successful operations, the fact remains that MacArthur was the general in charge, and as such, did an excellent job. He saved his reputation and made a new and better one as a conquering general.

This rehabilitation of his scarred reputation marked a real renascence in his own character as well. He was pompous, blustery, imperious and egotistical – all of these things – but he did a fine job and he knew it. So did Roosevelt and Marshall, who, vexed by his querulousness in 1942 and 1943, recognized his military abilities and gave him what he needed when they could. On the other hand, his political acumen left a lot to be desired. His understanding of American politics was naive, not to put too fine a point on it. Although he cannot be blamed for the way he handled the Bonus Marchers, since he was acting under the strict instructions of his superiors, he seemed to overestimate the influence of sinister and subversive forces among the Marchers. He was a man of the extreme right in the political spectrum, but as long as he stuck to military problems, this really did not seem to matter. All generals have an authoritarian streak; otherwise they would not be generals. MacArthur carried this authoritarian image to extremes. When first in Australia he tended to blame others for his short-comings, and did not understand or accept the decision to defeat Hitler first rather than Japan. His nagging of Washington, however, resulted in getting more men and supplies than he would have otherwise received and he put them to good use.

He was not reckless with men; his casualty record was low, and if the use of heavy firepower was required to win the war in the Pacific without an undue loss of life, then one can hardly criticize him for demanding more armaments, planes and ships. It was when his ego got the better of him, in the Philippine campaign, where he committed too many men to the reconquest of the archipelago when he should have concentrated on the conquest of Japan. But one has to return to his worst weakness – his belief in his own infallibility which was nurtured by a sycophantic staff which he kept around him. He made military mistakes, as all generals do, but he brooked no criticism. It was only when he ventured to self-criticize, when in Australia, that he was able to pull himself up by his own bootstraps and get down to the serious business of winning the war.

His taste for the melodramatic, one of his worst faults, actually aided him in his conduct of the Pacific war. His grandiose statements to the press appealed to the American people and helped build morale in the United States when the going was tough in the first months after America entered the war. Many generals would have been fired after a debacle such as MacArthur presided over in Bataan and Corregidor. MacArthur's prose saved his career. He was too popular to be dismissed, and through his own personal comeback, many Americans could live vicariously through his triumphs. His men may have resented his comments at times; but this resentment evolved into an attitude of grudging admiration for a general who would go ashore with his troops on many occasions, although he was a man in his 60s, even though they knew he did it as much to acquire public recognition for his own heroism as to build morale among his troops.

It was one thing for MacArthur to attack his Commander in Chief on military grounds; it is the duty of any officer to question the wisdom of his political masters when it comes to waging war. It is quite another thing to attack his President or Joint Chiefs of Staff on political grounds, where soldiers often are at their most vulnerable. Of all his weaknesses, this was MacArthur's worst, and it was to be painfully exposed in his postwar career which was marked by brilliance as Japan's new shogun as well as hesistancy and political ignorance as commander of the United Nations forces in Korea. It cannot erase his greatest qualities: his patriotism, his personal courage and his excellence as a military commander.

5:THE WARRIOR SHOGUN

When Douglas MacArthur stepped out on the deck of the battleship *Missouri* on the morning of 2 September 1945, he felt that he had been fully avenged. The honor of the United States had been cleansed of the humiliation of Bataan and Corregidor, and so had MacArthur's. He 'had returned' to the Philippines, despite a shocking loss of life during the 1944–45 Philippine campaign, not only of Americans and Filipinos but especially of Japanese. Now the final triumph: the acceptance of the unconditional surrender of Japan.

World War II was over, and for MacArthur, perhaps his military career. Although as Supreme Commander Allied Powers he had become the *de facto* ruler of Japan, MacArthur felt that, at the age of 65, he would complete his long and distinguished military career by overseeing the reconstruction of Japan. He was not to know that the most controversial phase of his military career would take place in those last years, which were to end, not in glory, but in humiliation once more.

MacArthur's six years in Japan ended in controversy which has not yet been fully resolved. If one looks at Japan in 1945 – a land wholly devastated, its cities razed to the ground, its economy in ruins, its people humiliated and desperate – and contrasts it with Japan in the 1970s – the third largest industrial power in the world with one of the world's strongest currencies, a democracy which, despite Japan's earlier traditions, has worked, and all of this achieved without an economy devoted to arms production, colonization or exploitation of its own people – the extent of MacArthur's influence cannot be overestimated. He above anyone else, helped to create the Japan of the 1970s. Therefore, when one regards MacArthur's six years in Japan, one must take into account his

not inconsiderable successes as well as his failures as a military campaigner and as a politician in postwar America.

The Japan which the Allies occupied in the late summer of 1945 was a frightened and confused nation. For almost a thousand years the warrior class had been revered by the Japanese. Only during World War I did Japan have her first commoner (that is, non-*samurai* class) as Prime Minister, and Hara Kei's ministry ended unhappily in his assassination in 1921. The period between the wars witnessed the growing impotence of the civil ministries in their rivalry with the two major branches of the military, so that, by late 1941, when Tojo Hideki became Premier, the military had, in effect, taken over civil authority in the name of the Emperor. World War II in the Pacific was caused largely by the growing influence of the imperialistic military class over the whole of society. Thus, despite the attempts to reform Japan in the 19th century, Japan on the eve of Pearl Harbor was still heavily influenced, if not controlled, by the military, even though it was no longer strictly speaking a hereditary class as it had been during the Tokugawa Period (1600–1868). If MacArthur had any specific aims when he took over Japan in 1945, one of them certainly was the elimination of the military in Japan as an independent force.

In August and September 1945 most Japanese were not terribly concerned with the new political order. They were dazed. Their locus of authority had crumbled. The Emperor's broadcast announcing the capitulation was a shock in itself. In it the inviolable, venerated Showa Emperor, Hirohito, announced to his people that they must '... endure the unendurable and suffer the insufferable.' Capitulation was to be immediate and complete. The Japanese looked now to their conquerors for direction and, in particular, to MacArthur, who, as Supreme Commander Allied Powers (SCAP), was to be their new leader. More than anything they looked to MacArthur as a symbol of hope and

Left: Admiral William Halsey, Lt Gen Robert Eichelberger and MacArthur salute the American flag at a ceremony in Tokyo at the US Embassy, the first flag raised over it since Pearl Harbor.

Above: MacArthur visits the ruins of his prewar residence, the Manila Hotel. The hotel has been returned to its former glory, and one can stay at the MacArthur Suite.

mercy, but at the same time feared retribution and revenge at the hands of the occupying armies.

MacArthur saw his task as one of replacing ancient Japanese institutions with carbon copies of American ones as MacArthur understood them. Instinctively a conservative both in politics and in his understanding of economics, he was not prepared to abolish all to rebuild. He respected the Japanese way of life and hoped to merge 'the best of theirs with the best of ours.'

To achieve his ambitious program confidence in his command had to be created from the start and a meeting with the Emperor was arranged in order to calm the fears of the Japanese people, many of whom feared total or partial enslavement under the new American command. MacArthur was uneasy about a meeting with the Emperor as he felt photographs of himself with Hirohito would make a martyr of the Emperor in the eyes of the people. Rather, he preferred to wait until the Emperor invited him voluntarily, but this invitation soon came and MacArthur accepted that the meeting would take place in the American Embassy rather than in the Imperial Palace.

MacArthur wanted to make certain that the Emperor would not be treated as a supplicant pleading a case for his people. Every honor which was due to a head of state would be his. MacArthur feared that the Emperor might feel that he had to plead for his life, for many of the Allies, especially the Russians and to some extent the British, sought his indictment as a war criminal. MacArthur strongly resisted these proposals, one of which was suggested by President Truman but quickly withdrawn. MacArthur believed that some continuity with the old order must be maintained for the sake of the Japanese people. To have their Emperor reduced from godhead to constitutional monarch was shocking enough. To have him tried or even executed would certainly have proved counterproductive to American efforts to conciliate their former enemy.

Hirohito's attitude was conciliatory and even penitent. He read out a statement to the General: 'I come to you, General MacArthur, to offer myself to the judgment of the powers you represent as the one to bear sole responsibility for every political and military decision made and action taken by my people in the conduct of the war.' MacArthur was enormously impressed by the courage of the once god-king. Expecting humiliation, the Emperor showed humility and inner strength. His reward was respect and courtesy returned in kind. Subsequent meetings between the two men indicated that MacArthur, who had approved a War Crimes Tribunal similar to that set up at Nuremberg to judge Japan's wartime leadership, would not countenance bringing the Emperor's name forward despite the pressures brought to bear on him to do so. The Emperor consistently supported MacArthur's policy of reconstruction.

In January 1946 the Emperor shocked his people by formally renouncing his divinity, which MacArthur felt was vital as a first step to democratize the authoritarian state. MacArthur has often been criticized for his own authoritarian stance toward politics and particularly to those who surrounded him, but in this instance there can be no doubt; MacArthur sought from the very outset of the occupation to bring Japan back to the family of nations as a democratic and peaceful state, removing the authoritarian influences of the past so as to prevent another outbreak of aggressive Japanese nationalism in the future. The first postwar Japanese Premier, Yoshida Shigeru, stated that MacArthur's respectful attitude toward the Emperor was the most important factor in making the occupation a success as well as bringing Japan back to democracy.

MacArthur's policy, therefore, was one of a benevolent despot who was going to bring about reconstruction and reform through his own initiative and under American tutelage rather than with the help and advice of the other wartime Allies. The Soviets as well as the British sought very early on to diminish MacArthur's power. They believed that like Germany and Austria, Japan should be divided into zones of responsibility. MacArthur felt, and subsequent events proved, that the

Above: MacArthur and Eichelberger (left) arrive by jeep at Malay Balay in the Philippines during an inspection tour of the 31st Infantry Division in June 1945.

division of these two countries was far less efficient than had been hoped. MacArthur's attitude was simple. He believed that the Allies' role in postwar Japan should therefore be in proportion to the wartime role, which was negligible. Furthermore, the US was supplying 75 percent of the occupying force.

MacArthur was not consulted when the Moscow Conference was held in December 1945 to discuss the postwar reconstruction of Japan, but the decisions reached did not wholly disappoint him. A Far Eastern Commission was authorized and consisted of all 11 nations who had fought against Japan in the war. The US surrendered its unilateral authority to the commission, but it was to meet in Washington at regular intervals and transmit its orders to an advisory group which was composed of the US, the British Commonwealth, China and the Soviet Union. This body met in Tokyo to oversee MacArthur's regime. Despite MacArthur's initial objections to this curtailment of his supreme authority, he soon realized that the composition of the advisory group was too diverse in its conceptual framework to be at all effective.

MacArthur's team was all-American, usually made up of wartime colleagues. Willoughby, MacArthur's German-born aide throughout the war, remained Chief of Intelligence, and served as the foremost propaganda agent of the occupation. General Courtney Whitney headed the so-called 'government section.' To this team was added William J Sebald in 1947, who became MacArthur's trusted assistant in political matters and in terms of liaison with Washington. Former aides like Sutherland and Diller were removed, with Major General Paul J Mueller replacing Sutherland as the Chief of Staff. In his memoirs MacArthur hardly mentions his departed aides, and the assumption is that personal disagreements were the chief reason for their replacement. MacArthur believed that personal loyalty came first

Below: MacArthur and General Joseph ('Vinegar Joe') Stilwell return the salute of guards as they leave General Headquarters in Manila.

Above: Lt Gen Temoyuki Yamashita led the Japanese drive to Singapore in 1941–42 and was tried before the War Crimes Tribunal in 1948 for his atrocities in the Philippines.

and foremost, and one of the main characteristics of loyalty was defined as subservience to the will of the Commander in Chief. Most of his staff were soldiers or men holding some sort of military rank. Thus, although the Allied Council was a thorn in MacArthur's side and gave the appearance of international control, the occupation of Japan was largely in MacArthur's hands. MacArthur chose to ignore the Council, although it provided a very useful forum where occupation policy could be criticized and discussed more openly by the Japanese than in any other body.

As the occupation continued a rift between MacArthur and his superiors in Washington became apparent. It was a rift which continued to widen. MacArthur interpreted his brief from Washington and even specific directives very broadly, and officials back home were more often than not confronted with *faits accomplis* rather than requests for consultation. MacArthur had had such a wide brief in the war, that he felt that he could continue along the same lines in peacetime. This was made easier for him by the President, Harry S Truman, whose personal fear and hatred of Communism was shared by MacArthur. Both men wanted to see Japan quickly rebuilt as a democratic and pro-Western state. However, Truman was not the ideologue that MacArthur was on the subject of international Communism. MacArthur felt that Communism was another insidious form of pan-Slavism and imperialism under the

guise of a working-class solidarity. Truman tended to view the postwar world in power-political terms. Both interpreted international Communism to be a monolith under the leadership of Stalin, and in 1947 who could have doubted this assertion? Mao Tse-tung's Chinese Communists were being given limited Soviet aid, but at first did not seem to pose such an over-weening threat to the renewed and rehabilitated Nationalist government of MacArthur's friend, Chiang Kai-shek. The states of Eastern Europe were clearly under Moscow's control, but the quasi-independent, nationalist-cum-communist movements in Southeast Asia, such as that of Ho Chi Minh, were not yet important.

It was not until Greece and Turkey seemed to be in imminent danger of falling to Communist governments that Truman took positive action by implementing the so-called Truman Doctrine of 1947. Certainly he was less optimistic than Roosevelt that the US could 'handle' Stalin, and disappointments over Poland and Berlin were only two of the examples that Truman gave in his memoirs of Soviet perfidy over the implementation of the Yalta and Potsdam agreements. Truman did not overreact when Czechoslovakia was taken over by the Communists in early 1948. Until the Berlin Blockade Truman did little except encourage governments in Western Europe to withstand Soviet pressures and to curtail the powers of Communist parties within some of these states, notably Italy and France until the promulgation of the Marshall Plan in 1947.

The rebuilding of Japan was of primary importance. Stalin had once boasted that 'with Japan, we are invincible.' MacArthur agreed that this was largely true, and was therefore determined to see that Soviet influence be kept out of Japan at all costs. Thus, his opposition to the Allied Commission was based on his objection to the Soviet representative on it. He believed that Truman was naive, if not severely misguided, to have even taken a conciliatory attitude toward Soviet aggression. In short, MacArthur was a right-winger to his fingertips, and used his influence as an American military hero of World War II to make contact with right-wing Republican interests in the United States who shared MacArthur's view of Truman. Ideological fervor was MacArthur's strength

as well as his greatest weakness. He had respected Roosevelt, but any respect he had for his successor initially faded once Truman had been in office a few months. The origins of the Truman-MacArthur split are to be found in Truman's insistence that occupation policy be made in Washington, not in MacArthur's headquarters at the Dai-Ichi Building in Tokyo. As long as it was only occupation policy that was in question, Truman and MacArthur did not openly clash. In the interim MacArthur's nascent distrust for civilian authority and disrespect for Truman in particular continued to smolder.

Below: Roosevelt and Churchill confer with Generalissimo Chiang Kai-Shek and Madame Chiang at the Cairo Conference in 1943.

Despite his attitude toward Washington and most members of the American press, whom he tried to ignore whenever possible, MacArthur's leadership in post-war Japan was effective. It is difficult to imagine a better choice of individual to have taken up the almost insuperable task of rebuilding Japan both morally and physically in order to create a stable nation tied politically and economically to the United States. Choosing him as a latter-day shogun, to act for an Emperor without real power, was one of those fortunate accidents of history when the right man is chosen to do a job which, in retrospect, seemed destined for him from the beginning of his career. MacArthur was imperious, vain and decisive. He was also courageous and forthright – qualities which the

Below: Ho Chi Minh, known as Nguyen Ai Quoc during the war, was returned by the Americans to a position of authority in Vietnam as the British took the Japanese surrender there in Sept-Oct 1945.

Japanese people admired above all others. They needed a father figure to lead them, and MacArthur's paternalism was perfect at the time. Edwin O Reischauer, one of America's greatest historians of Japan, was never one of MacArthur's greatest admirers yet his summary of MacArthur as Supreme Commander Allied Powers stands as a lasting tribute to what must be called MacArthur's finest period:

'His flair for the dramatic, his thundering phrases, his appreciation of the tremendous historical significance of his own acts, all had a strong emotional appeal to the Japanese. Here was a leader who combined emotional depth with firmness of will. General MacArthur became to the Japanese the symbol of perfection, the inspired leader, the knight in shining armor, and they repaid him, foreign conqueror though he was, with unlimited respect and often enough with adulation.'

Disarming a vast military machine of over 7,000,000 was not an easy task, but it was accomplished swiftly and without great difficulties. Repatriation of Japanese troops was accomplished equally smoothly, although some remained in occupation of many parts of Southeast Asia for as long as several months after the capitulation. The Potsdam Declaration had ordered that Japan be totally disarmed, and it was toward this that MacArthur worked. The dangers inherent in this policy and the reversal of it were not to become apparent at once. Hundreds of thousands of Japanese citizens, not all of them connected with the old military regime, were prevented from holding public office. It was MacArthur's desire, as well as that of the Allies, to demilitarize Japanese society from top to bottom, as well as to destroy the power and position of the *zaibatsu*, the small group of family companies which controlled almost all of Japan's industrial strength. Leading members of these families were earmarked for trial before a war crimes commission along with the military leaders whom many had opposed right up to the outbreak of World War II in the Pacific. Potsdam had declared that 'stern justice shall be meted out to all war criminals, including those who have visited cruelties upon our prisoners.'

General Yamashita, who had fought so cruelly and effectively against Mac-

Arthur during the Philippine campaign, was among the first to be executed. His case, in the light of subsequent events, was a crucial test. Yamashita had fought to the bitter end, taking hundreds of thousands of lives in the name of his country. He argued and eventually appealed to the US Supreme Court that he had only done his duty as a soldier, despite the severities and horrors which were perpetrated by many of his men. His appeal was rejected, and President Truman backed MacArthur's decision that he should be among the first to die.

General Homma's case was far more clear cut. Author of the Bataan Death March in 1942, he was already stripped of his officer's commission by the Emperor when the facts were revealed to him, and he was swiftly sentenced to death by the war crimes tribunal. Although his wife appealed to MacArthur to save him, MacArthur, who wanted Homma's scalp probably more than anyone else's, declared that if he did not deserve his fate, no one in 'jurisdictional history ever did.' His sentence was carried out under MacArthur's orders, and thereafter the International Military Tribunal for the Far East was allowed to render its decisions in due course.

The tribunal sat for three years, and although many were tried and sentenced outside Japan by the individual countries involved, the big show trial involved 25 major war criminals, who numbered among them four former prime ministers. Tojo, the mastermind behind Pearl Harbor, who was in power throughout most of the war, was sentenced to death, along with Hirota. Both were hanged, as well as five others. The rest were given prison sentences of varying duration. One of the most well-known of those imprisoned as a result of the trials was 'Tokyo Rose,' the alluring broadcaster to American troops during the war.

The drafting of a new constitution was another of the momentous duties which MacArthur was called upon to fulfil. Japan's first constitution had been promulgated in 1890. It had developed out of the Meiji Restoration of 1868, and had ensured that those who made the revolution which overthrew the shogunate and established a new regime in the name of the Emperor would be able to maintain their power over the state. The Emperor was defined

Above: British and Australian POWs at a lumber camp in Thailand during the building of the infamous Death Railway and the Bridge over the River Kwai. War crimes charges were brought against some of those responsible.

as being sacred and inviolable, and the structure of the new regime, based on a Prussian model, was highly authoritarian, leaving much of the power in the hands of the Genro, a council of elders, and in the hands of an independent military whose loyalty was to the Emperor alone and not to the elected authority. The upper house had at least equal power with a lower house which, at first, was elected by a narrowly-based constituency.

Since the Emperor declared himself no longer sacred after the war, the ideological underpinnings of the Meiji Constitution had been removed, and, in any event, the independent military had been abolished. A new constitution was needed. Both the US government and MacArthur believed that it should be drastically revised so as to ensure democratic government in future based

on universal suffrage. A committee was quickly formed by the vestigial Japanese government to draft a new constitution, but the Japanese asked for a path toward democracy be shown to them by their new masters. The first draft which was shown to MacArthur in January 1964 was little more than a rewording of the old Meiji Constitution. MacArthur was faced with a problem of timing. Elections, Japan's first for nearly a decade, were scheduled for 10 April 1946. MacArthur hoped that this election would be a sort of referendum on a new constitution, and he felt it imperative that it be written before election day.

Thus, unknown to the Japanese who were working on the constitution, MacArthur appointed Courtney Whitney to draft one with the help of his staff of military advisers. Within a month it was completed, and the Japanese authorities, notably Premier Shidehara, reluctantly accepted it. One clause, inserted at Shidehara's request, declared that the Japanese people would renounce war forever and would never maintain any sort of defense force. This article,

since the new constitution was put in effect there has been no real indication that his trust in the Japanese people not to repeat the errors of the past was unjustified.

In the elections the voters, which, for the first time, included women, seemed to approve the new constitution which is known euphemistically as the 'MacArthur Constitution.' Yoshida was elected Prime Minister, and the two newly-elected houses of the Diet approved it in due course. It became law on 3 November 1946, and went into effect in May 1947. The chief difference between the Meiji and the MacArthur constitutions is in the position of the Emperor, who was now simply the Head of State and symbol of the Japanese people – in short, a constitutional monarch along roughly British lines. There was a separation of powers as in the American constitution, with an independent judiciary, a supreme court, and a military (or self-defense) establishment firmly under the control of the bicameral legislature. A bill of rights guaranteeing civil liberties, freedom of speech and press was incorporated into the constitution, and the prime minister elected from the majority party in the lower house serves a four-year term

unless he receives a vote of no-confidence, which demands a new election. Elections for the Diet were to take place every four years. Amendment was made possible through national referenda. For the Japanese the most radical departure from past methods was the establishment of full universal suffrage. MacArthur was determined that Japanese women should abandon their long-subservient position in society and this was readily accepted, at least within the constitutional framework. This was probably the greatest change wrought by the MacArthur constitution. Certainly this hastily constructed document was not without its faults, but it was widely praised by Americans and Japanese alike at the time, including President Truman.

Despite the fact that it was an amalgam of British and American models drawn up with little Japanese assistance, it has subsequently worked well. Japan's democratic and political development has been a model since the war, despite the fact that it has not yet been given the supreme test: a change in government. The Liberal Party (which would better be described as Conservative in the British sense) has remained in power since 1947. There is little doubt that the Japanese constitution of 1947, like its West German counterpart, could sustain this change as and when it occurs. In any event, the position of women in Japan was forever altered, as much by

though conforming to the spirit and letter of the Potsdam Declaration, was impractical. The implication was that Japan would always be militarily defenseless, and with fears of the Soviet military and naval power immediately to the north and west of the Japanese islands. MacArthur saw that either American forces would have to remain in Japan permanently (obviously not a viable solution) or Japan would be exposed to presumed Soviet aggression immediately upon the withdrawal of the Americans. MacArthur therefore chose to interpret this clause as not preventing Japan from building up defense forces in future if she ever came 'within the orbit of immediate threatened attack.' This clause was therefore rendered quite meaningless. Japan should be either with armed forces or without them. MacArthur wanted them to arm for self-defense, but not for expansion, a fine point which left the doors wide open for a revival of Japanese armed imperialism. MacArthur knew the chance he was taking, but he believed it was necessary, and over the 35 years

Below: MacArthur alights from his C-54 *Bataan* on Japanese soil after the enemy's capitulation.

Left: Members of the Japanese surrender commission sign the surrender aboard the battleship USS *Missouri* on 2 Sept 1945.
Top: Lt Gen Kuzma N Dereyanko signs the surrender document aboard the *Missouri* on behalf of the Soviet Union.
Above: MacArthur and Sutherland watch as Japanese General Yoshira Umezu signs the surrender on behalf of Imperial General Headquarters.

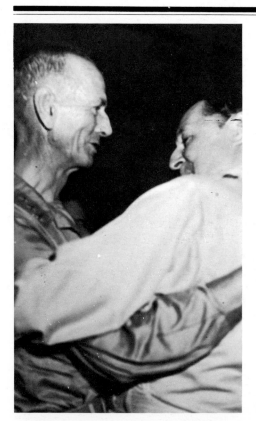

the war itself and the breakdown of Japanese society in general as by the new constitution.

Political reforms were only the beginning of the MacArthur regime; economic reforms were equally top priority for the Dai-Ichi staff. Top of the list at the beginning of the occupation was to feed a demoralized people whose means of food and goods production had been shattered. To this end MacArthur arranged for airlifts of food, but it was his firm intention to make Japan economically self-sufficient as quickly as possible. There can be little doubt that in this respect MacArthur's rehabilitation of Japan was an unqualified success. When the war ended Japan's economy was in severe trouble. Taxes had been in-

Left: MacArthur embraces his Corregidor colleague Wainwright after his release from prison camp.
Below: MacArthur, Wainwright, Percival, Sutherland, Blamey, Krueger and Dereyanko meet after the surrender.

creasingly heavy throughout the war, and money, by the end, was virtually worthless. Industrial production was down to about 10 percent of prewar levels, and what there was left was confined to turning used helmets into pots and pans and making wood pulp into ersatz cloth. Food was in desperately short supply: each person was allowed no more than 1000 calories a day, and many Japanese people were forced to live from what charity the American soldiers were prepared to give. In fact the occupying forces were very generous, as individuals as well as through the established authority. Housing was yet another serious problem. Those sound buildings left standing were soon commandeered by the American forces.

The occupation authorities did little to alleviate suffering initially. Recovery, from the Japanese point of view, was agonizingly slow. The problem of feeding, housing and clothing a vast population as well as rebuilding their once-

Above: MacArthur addresses a joint session of the Philippine Congress. The Philippines had been promised independence from the US, which they received in 1946.

great industrial machine was so vast as to prove almost impossible at first. Inflation was rife; prices rose at a rate of about 10 percent each month for the first two years of the occupation. Black market activities, not unexpectedly, were widespread, especially with the existence of American bases full to overflowing with badly needed goods. These activities were tacitly tolerated by both the Japanese and American authorities, as they were a help to those who were lucky enough to get some food. Profiteering and exploitation were widespread. The policy of removing 1100 industrial plants to the United States as part of a reparations program was soon abandoned, but while in effect, it made the grave situation worse.

The *zaibatsu*-busting policy adopted by MacArthur was almost as devastating as other early attempts to stabilize the Japanese economy. Initially the attempt to break up major Japanese cartels or trusts met no opposition; the principal holding companies were obliged to dispose of their stocks to the general public on the open market. The sales went into the hands of a Japanese government agency under the direction of SCAP, and this presented the first problem. The companies were denied control of their stocks from the very outset, even before the shares were sold. Antimonopoly laws similar to those in the US were soon adopted, and in the resulting confusion the rebuilding of industrial strength got off to a slow start. In retrospect, it is hard to see what all this activity was about. The Japanese economy, though not as tightly controlled by a few families as it was before the war, is still rigidly structured and directed by a few main companies, most of them offshoots or even continuations of the prewar combines. The American authorities were obsessed with the notion that the *zaibatsu* had somehow perpetrated the war. The opposite was more the case. Big business in Japan had tried to preserve democracy and fought off the military, its rivals for power, almost to the very outbreak of hostilities with America.

Deconcentration of economic power was all the more disastrous in the light of Japan's severe economic crisis. MacArthur soon recognized that the deconcentration program was not going to work, and soon the number of corporations to be dissolved was reduced from 1200 to 325, then to 30 and finally to nine. When these nine were broken up it was announced that the deconcentration program had been successfully completed. However, it would be an exaggeration to state that the *zaibatsu*-busting effort was a total failure. Some concentration of power was broken up. For example, Mitsui and Mitsubishi, two huge conglomerates, were broken up into some 240 separate companies. That this group of companies was reorganized about a decade later and soon came to resemble something like their prewar structure is another matter. The closed nature of the Japanese economic system was opened up for a time and competition on a Western model was a

refreshing, if temporary change in major industry. The *zaibatsu* were and probably still are necessary for Japan's industrial expansion. They were done a great favor by the war, for they were forced to concentrate their postwar economic thrust in the area of goods for domestic consumption rather than for military uses, and the reorganization of Japanese industry allowed Japan to smoothly move into high gear, once the initial problems had been overcome.

MacArthur's most important economic reform was to foster a trade union movement. Before the war Japan had been tightly controlled by the military, government and big business, and collective bargaining on an American model was more or less unknown. MacArthur encouraged labor unions to form as a counterpoise to his attempt to break up the *zaibatsu*, and as early as 1947 there were about 25,000 unions in Japan with roughly 5,000,000 members. MacArthur was undoubtedly a right-winger politically, but this did not prevent him from fostering a movement which is usually associated with left-wing politics but which he recognized as being necessary for Japan's industrial growth. However,

Communist elements infiltrated some of the unions, and when a general strike was called MacArthur called upon the military to threaten action. From that point on strikers and labor demonstrators clashed frequently with Japanese police and American military police and even, on occasion, US combat troops. In 1948 MacArthur revised the Trade Union Law which he had promulgated in 1945 to restrict some union excesses along the lines of the American Taft-Hartley Act, and this action was soon followed by a McCarthy-like purge of leading Japanese unions of Communist-affiliated leaders, driving them underground.

The confidence many workers had in the American occupation forces was shattered by this action, and it was widely felt that the working class had been betrayed by the United States. This in turn played into the hands of Communist elements, who now could portray themselves as the only true representatives of the working class in Japan. Japanese labor was subsequently wedded to radicalism. This anomaly can only be explained through an American lack of understanding of Japanese labor relations before the war. Although MacArthur genuinely desired to see a free labor union movement, he had envisaged its development along essentially American lines, that is to say, loyal, patriotic and fundamentally conserva-

tive in its outlook. The American labor-management relationship is virtually unique among the Western countries, and it would have been unrealistic to expect it to work in a similar way in Japan. However, it would be an exaggeration to say that American policy toward the trade unions in Japan was a failure. Since the war Japan's labor-management relations have been tempestuous but, on the whole, stable, if paternalistic. Japan's economic growth since the war has been spectacular and largely unhindered by strikes and labor unrest. No general strike actually took place, either during the occupation or since. In retrospect, MacArthur's policy seems enlightened, if at first somewhat unrealistic in the Japanese context.

Perhaps MacArthur's greatest achievement during the occupation years was in the field of land reform. With the approval of SCAP the Japanese government passed the Farm Reform Law in October 1946. Before the war the feudal-like system of landholding prevalent during the Tokugawa Period had not altered greatly since the Meiji Restoration. Peasant farmers were closely tied to the land they tilled, few owned land

outright, and most were tenant farmers who were forced to pay high rents (in terms of their incomes) to absentee landlords. MacArthur believed in the old American principle that he who tills the soil should own it. For the former tenants this policy was an unexpected windfall. Over 2,000,000 peasants became landholders virtually overnight when the government bought up the land from the former landlords at ridiculously low prices (roughly the equivalent of the black market price for a carton of cigarettes per acre) and then resold it to the peasants at equally low terms, which could be payable in installments over a 33-year period at 3.2 percent interest. This transfer of property came at a time when whatever an agricultural worker produced was eagerly absorbed by a food-starved economy, much of it through the more profitable black market channels. Landlords were obviously hard-hit initially, and many individuals suffered personal tragedies.

Below: MacArthur at the daily ceremony of his leaving his SCAP headquarters at the Dai-Ichi Building in Tokyo. Usually hundreds of Japanese watched him leave.

Nevertheless, as a social class the former landlords managed well and somehow survived, but the social implications of the land reform were profound. Over 5,000,000 acres were transferred to former tenants, and the farmers came into their own as a stable, strongly capitalist force in society.

By 1970 over 10 percent of all arable land was still held in tenancy, and cash rentals were controlled by law. A large acreage of land outside the main urban centers was converted into suburbia, and peasants who came to own that land after the war found themselves in their middle- or old-age as rich landlords of blocks of flats or offices. The inflation spiral which the war and occupation precipitated was dramatic in land prices, especially near Japanese cities, and farmers were made rich or at least well-to-do as a result of MacArthur's land reform. Agricultural productivity soared, and Japan ceased to be economically dependent on other countries for its food supply. Many more acres were brought under cultivation during and after the occupation, and although MacArthur's policy cannot take all the credit, at least one can safely say that it began a pro-

cess which has resulted in economic prosperity for the cultivator and for the country as a whole.

Part of the credit must go to the United States government as well, which poured in about 200,000,000 dollars in economic aid. This was, admittedly, a much smaller amount than was given to the major industrial states of Western Europe after the war, but there is a good reason why this relatively small amount of aid was utilized so well. The long occupation of Japan forced the expenditure of these funds to be wisely planned. Japan had a vast storehouse of technical know-how, and experienced scientists, engineers and business entrepreneurs could take advantage of American aid at once. Although there was bound to be a certain amount of graft involved in any vast operation of this kind, it was kept to a minimum by MacArthur's strict husbanding of funds, and thus produced maximum benefit for the country. This sort of strict accounting was not possible in countries receiving far more aid, such as France and Great Britain, who were, after all, independent allies to be treated with a large measure of deference. MacArthur's cost control as

Above: MacArthur greets Manuel Roxas, the new President of the Philippines, upon his arrival in Manila on 2 July 1946 to celebrate Philippine independence declared two days later.

well as the genius of the Japanese people themselves are responsible for Japan's economic miracle in the 1950s and 1960s; from a state of economic ruin Japan has now become the third largest industrial machine in the world and has one of the world's strongest economies.

The export boom in domestic products began during the occupation and accelerated after the Korean War. New buildings rose everywhere; a real estate boom was in full swing by 1949. Shops were overflowing with every type of domestic goods, streets recently rebuilt were jammed to overflowing with new cars, some of them built by a nascent automobile industry, Japanese owned and operated, which has now become a major competitor of West German and American car manufacturers. The construction of motorways soon began. If anything industrial growth has been too successful, and changes in the environmental balance were disregarded. The physical appearance of Japan inevitably had to change because of wartime destruction, but perhaps in their desire to rebuild quickly Japanese traditional values have taken a back seat to economic progress. But there can be no question about the fact that MacArthur helped more than anyone else to begin the reconstruction of Japanese society.

At least as significant as his economic and political reforms were the fundamental social changes wrought by MacArthur's educational reforms. MacArthur was deeply concerned about this aspect of Japanese life for a number of reasons. As an American, MacArthur believed that control over primary and secondary education should be in the hands of local authorities in order to preserve the regional character of education as well as to prevent dictation from an ideologically-oriented, distant capital. This practice was not common to Japan at any time in its recent history. A ministry of education purchased school books on a national basis, and of course during the war not only education, but press, radio, films and theaters were under the control of a propaganda ministry. Nevertheless Japanese education, not only before the war, but over a century ago, was among the best in the world. When Perry first visited Japan in the middle of the 19th century about 46 percent of all adult males were literate. This figure compares very favorably with every country in the world at that time, including the United States. After the Meiji Restoration the Imperial Rescript on Education set the tone for the next half century. As early as 1872 attendance at primary schools was made compulsory for all children, at a time when universal compulsory education was merely a concept in most Western countries. This policy was expanded in later years when existing universities were made larger and new universities, both public and private, were founded. By the 1930s Japan's educational system, on the surface, was second to none in the world. But it had a grave fault. It was designed, not so much for the improvement of the individual, but for the training of that individual in the service of the state, as well as society. Thus education was strictly controlled by the national government so that students of every variety were molded into one regimented, standardized mold, with originality and initiative suffering as a result. Utilitarian studies, such as engineering and the physical sciences were stressed at the expense of literature and the arts. Dissatisfaction with the system was widespread among many Japanese educators even before the war, but when the teaching of Shinto propaganda became widespread immediately before and during the war, their voices were silenced. Once defeat was grudgingly accepted, it was obvious that there was a groundswell of support for radical changes in Japan's educational system. However, there was great controversy about how it could be changed.

Soon after his arrival in Japan MacArthur suspended the teaching of geography, history, the martial sports and particularly 'ethics,' which was an important outlet for the dissemination of nationalist and Shinto-oriented propaganda. Meanwhile a US Education Mission composed of 27 prominent American educators was sent to Japan under the leadership of Dr George D Stoddard, subsequently President of the University of Illinois. It spent only three weeks in Japan and then presented a report to General MacArthur. Few of the educators were familiar with Japan, but despite the hurried nature of their report, it was quite balanced and constructive in tone. It suggested a decentralization of Japan's educational system and its dispersal among autonomous, locally elected education authorities on the American model. New textbooks were quickly published to replace their nationalistic predecessors.

Many problems unforeseen by MacArthur soon appeared. Though it had been centralized, the Japanese education authority had been competent and professional. Many of these bureaucrats in Tokyo now found their authority usurped by petty officials on the local level who knew little and cared less for education as such. The restructuring of the school system into primary, junior high schools, high schools and universities on American lines was successful in that many more students had the opportunity to pursue their individual interests in formal educational institutions in adulthood. Massive expansion of educational opportunity implies a watering down of education for all. In any event some of the local authority was gradually undermined by Tokyo over the years, but there can be no doubt that there is a wider range of choice for the individual student than before the war and that freedom of expression is far more prevalent than in the past. MacArthur deserves the credit he has received from most Japanese for his work in reforming the educational system.

MacArthur's penchant for reform was given expression in many other ways. He saw to it that 70,000,000 people were vaccinated for smallpox within the first three years of the occupation. Over 23,000,000 people were vaccinated for tuberculosis, and that disease was reduced considerably as a result. Cholera, thanks to widespread inoculation, was virtually abolished by 1947. All these diseases had been endemic to Japan at one time or other, and epidemics had plagued the country well into the 20th

Below: MacArthur leaves his offices in Tokyo on the day he announced that he would be willing to run for the American Presidency if nominated.

century. Dysentery was almost wiped out, as was typhoid and paratyphoid.

Taken all in all, despite temporary setbacks in the first stages of the occupation, by 1949 Japan had been transformed. The *New York Times,* never one of MacArthur's greatest supporters, said that 'Japan is the one bright spot in Allied military government. General MacArthur's administration is a model of government and a boon to peace in the Far East.' Most Japanese shared this view. More than anything else, however, MacArthur's presence and his flair for the dramatic touched the Japanese people at a time when they needed understanding and inspiration.

MacArthur returned to the Philippines, the scene of some of his greatest triumphs and disasters, in 1946 to celebrate the establishment of the former American dominion as an independent state. This was one of the few times that MacArthur's name hit the headlines in the United States since the end of the war.

His reforms in Japan were largely unknown to the wider American public, and, in any event, attention was naturally turned toward internal affairs such as housing, the end of rationing, the economic boom, labor disputes and other domestic matters once most of the boys were brought back home from the war. The Democratic Party and Harry S Truman in particular came under heavy attack in 1946 and 1947. In the midterm elections of November 1946 a Republican Congress was returned to Washington for the first time since the onset of the Great Depression. Truman, who fought the railroad strikers to a standstill and who had demobilized something like 14,000,000 men, came under severe criticism. America was weary of war and foreign affairs and longed for a leader with a more dignified style.

General Dwight D Eisenhower, MacArthur's counterpart in Europe, was often mentioned in 1947 and early 1948 as a possible contender for both the

Above: General and Mrs MacArthur pictured at an air base near Tokyo after the general returned from Formosa following talks with the Chinese Nationalists and Chiang Kai-shek.

Democratic and Republican nominations for President. The Southern wing of the Democratic Party opposed Truman because of his pro-civil rights stance; the left-wing of the Party opposed his increasingly belligerent policy toward the Soviet Union. Both could unite under the war hero, Eisenhower, whose political opinions were known only to himself. The Democrats needed him more than the Republicans if the almost unprecedented act of 'dumping a President' (refusing to nominate a man in their party who already held the office) was to succeed. The Republicans, if they failed to get Ike, had a man after their own heart in Douglas MacArthur. His views were solidly right-wing; his affiliation with the Republican Party unquestioned. Although he denies in his memoirs that he wanted the nomination, MacArthur would have liked nothing better than to move from virtual dictator of Japan to the Presidency of the United States. This was what many Americans feared. Although he was widely admired

as a military hero, MacArthur had a wide critical audience as well. He made no bones about the fact that he opposed most of the New Deal legislation of the 1930s and his quarrels with Roosevelt before and during the war were not a closely guarded secret. Thus, when his name was put forward as a candidate for the Wisconsin primary election in April 1948, his coyness fooled no one. He was soundly rejected at the polls, and the right-wing of the Republican Party mobilized behind Senator Robert A Taft of Ohio. MacArthur was deeply disappointed by the outcome of his short-lived candidacy, even though he had stated that he was not a candidate. More than that, MacArthur bitterly resented the criticism he underwent in the campaign about his conduct as SCAP. Surrounded by sycophants in Tokyo, MacArthur was not used to the cut and thrust of stateside politics. He began to nurse a long-standing grudge against Washington which he had developed throughout the war and into the Japanese occupation. He felt that not only did the American people not understand his point of view; the President and the Joint Chiefs of Staff shared the same misconceptions. These alleged mis-

conceptions were not particularly relevant to home affairs, with which MacArthur had been out of touch since he left for the Philippines in 1935.

MacArthur's feelings about Far Eastern affairs in 1948 and 1949 were a mixture of disappointment and frustration because of his lack of control over developments outside his authority in Japan. He approved of Philippine independence, but of little else. Chagrin turned to near pathological rage as he helplessly watched Chiang Kai-shek's regime being systematically overrun by the Chinese Communists. American policy toward the Nationalists was to attempt to forge some sort of working relationship between them and the Communists. The Marshall Mission had as its aim to bring about the formation of a coalition government between the two opposing forces. Despite Marshall's temporary success at maneuvering a truce of several months' duration in 1946, both sides recognized this as merely a pause before yet another round of fighting, a time to regroup forces and to amass arms. The American government, meanwhile, saw to it that the major cities of coastal China were handed over to the Kuomintang (KMT) as Japanese occupying forces surrendered to them.

MacArthur believed, as Harry Hopkins, Roosevelt's aide, did, that by taking an uncompromising attitude toward the Communists and by giving maximum material aid to the Chinese Nationalists, the United States could ensure the establishment of a friendly government in mainland China. This attitude, widely held in 1945, was totally unrealistic. Despite the massive amounts of assistance the Nationalists received during the war, they refused to commit their troops to meaningful engagements against the Japanese who occupied most of coastal China. Chiang Kai-shek foresaw the defeat of Japan by the Allies without his help, and recognized Mao Tse-tung as his principal enemy. The regime was misshapen and corrupt. Hundreds of millions of dollars were squandered and grafted away by KMT during the war. By refusing to engage the Japanese in any significant way, Chiang had lost much of the support he once commanded among the Chinese people. When fighting resumed at the end of 1946, Chiang had only one hope – to remain in control of the situation, retain territory and maintain internal stability. He failed to do this. The Communists quickly seized Manchuria and began operating from there and from their Yenan base in northwest China, conducting widespread guerrilla activities against the Kuomintang regime, while, at the same time, pushing Chiang's forces southward.

MacArthur never supported the idea that American troops be sent to defend Chiang, but he hoped that the US would send more aid. In fact three billion dollars were spent on Chiang. It was not enough. No amount would have been. When the Communists entered Peking in 1949 it was clear that the Mandate of Heaven in China had been lost by Chiang. By the end of the year the remnants of Chiang's Nationalist Army were in Formosa, where Chiang continued to maintain his regime, while Mao Tse-tung controlled all of mainland China. MacArthur reluctantly accepted this situation and in a press interview on 1 March

Above: Bomb damage in the center of
Kobe pictured late in 1945.
Left: Flooded drydock at Kure with
damaged midget submarines. The
reconstruction of devastated cities and
industrial plant was one of MacArthur's
most pressing problems in postwar Japan.

1949 he defined America's new line of
defense against Communism – from
Alaska through Japan to the Philippines.
America, in his view, was not to commit
itself to the defense of the continent of
Asia, but would maintain a defense perimeter based on sea and air power.

MacArthur's authority in Korea
gradually faded and was finally curtailed.
According to the Potsdam agreement,
the United States was to occupy the
southern half of the Korean peninsula
up to the 38th Parallel while the Russians were to move down to that line
from their positions in Eastern Siberia
and Manchuria. This procedure was
followed and MacArthur received the
Japanese surrender in the more popu-
lous half of Korea in 1945. He was given
responsibility for the American troops
in the area. North Korea had a population of about 9,000,000 against the
south's 21,000,000. North Korea had
most of what was left of Korea's industrial machine, whereas the south was
largely an agricultural region.

The concept in 1945 was that the
two Koreas would be joined after elections were held. The General Assembly
of the United Nations decided to establish a UN Commission to supervise these
elections in November 1947. The Soviets, however, refused to allow the
Commission to operate in North Korea,
and the Soviet puppet government of
Kim Il Sung claimed sovereignty over
the whole of the country. So did Syngman Rhee, the provisional president of
the southern half, and so when elections
were finally held in 1948 they covered
only the southern (American occupied)
half of the peninsula. On 15 August 1948
the Republic of Korea was formally
proclaimed in the south, and MacArthur
attended the inauguration ceremonies
on one of his few trips away from Tokyo
during the years of the occupation. In his

Above: Joseph Stalin tried to convince the Allies that a partition of Japan should take place in which Russia would seize the northern island of Hokkaido.

Above: Mao Tse-tung took over most of northern China after the Japanese and Russians evacuated the area, before his final struggle against the Nationalists.

speech MacArthur urged that the barrier between the two halves of the country be quickly torn down, although by now it had become clear to all that the demarcation line of the 38th Parallel was now, in effect, an international boundary. North Korea, aided immeasurably by the Soviet Union, built up a formidable military machine while, at the same time, the Americans prepared for their withdrawal from South Korea.

The American government's attitude toward Korea since the end of the war was clear; it was not considered part of America's defense perimeter. The Joint Chiefs of Staff advised the State Department in September 1947 that the US had 'little strategical interest in maintaining the present troops and bases in Korea.' On the advice of the Joint Chiefs, President Truman approved a statement in April 1948 indicating that any action taken in Korea by either side would not constitute a *casus belli* for the United States. As a result the troops were withdrawn by 1949 and MacArthur's responsibility in Korea came to an end. All that was left was a military advisory group, 480 strong, whose purpose was to assist in the training of Korean military forces. Secretary of State, Dean Acheson, announced to the National Press Club in

Washington on 12 January 1950 his definition of America's new defense perimeter in Asia. It stretched from Alaska through Japan to the Philippines. No mention was made of either Korea or Formosa. It seemed on the surface, at least, that Truman, Acheson, the Joint Chiefs and MacArthur were at one on this point.

This was not really the case. MacArthur maintained intelligence units in Korea, and he was informed by his aide, Willoughby, that a massive build up of armed forces was taking place in North Korea, forces which were far in excess of those the United States had left in the south. The South Korean army numbered just under 100,000. In addition there was a local constabulary of 48,000 as well as a small coast guard detachment, in all less than 8000. There were no tanks, no fighter or bomber aircraft, no heavy artillery, only some field artillery, small arms, mortars and some anti-tank guns. In short, not enough to withstand an attack for more than a few days at most. The North Korean army, supplied with Soviet arms and a sizeable number of Soviet advisers, numbered 135,000 men, many of whom had served in the Chinese Communist army during World War II. There was an armored

brigade of some 6000 men equipped with 120 Russian medium tanks mounting 85mm guns. In June 1950 the North Korean air force had 40 fighters, 70 bombers, and some 180 planes in all. There were negligible naval forces present in the north but there was a Soviet-trained local constabulary of another 1800 men.

The Assembly of the Republic of Korea, which recognized the imminent danger once American troops were removed in late June 1949, asked for further assistance, but it was not forthcoming. The Russians had by then withdrawn all their regular forces from Korea, and the State Department, now in charge of Korean affairs once the troops under MacArthur had been removed, did not seriously consider the possibility of a successful armed attack from the north. Even as late as June 1950 John Foster Dulles, who was helping to prepare a peace treaty with Japan and who visited MacArthur in Tokyo, went to Korea as the personal representative of Dean Acheson. Only a couple of weeks before the war broke out he saw and was told nothing that led him to believe that any sort of attack was imminent. Significantly, however, Dulles told the National Assembly of South Korea that if they were attacked at some point in future, the United States would support them.

An inconsistency in American policy toward Formosa and Korea is evident here. On the one hand, in the years leading up to 1950 every important observer of the situation in East Asia concluded that since the Communists had overrun China, there was no point in denying them the whole of Chinese territory as defined in the Yalta and Potsdam settlements; that is to say, since Formosa, once a Japanese colony, was clearly going to be returned to China in the peace treaty with Japan once it was signed, it should not be denied to whatever government was in power in China, Nationalist or Communist. The Americans had also stated that Korea was not within the American defense perimeter, either by implication or explicitly. MacArthur, never enthusiastic about either policy, reluctantly had to accede publicly to the opinion of the President, the State Department and the Pentagon. His private opinions were cynical. He felt that the Dulles speech indicated a switch in policy. It is necessary to go behind the scenes to examine the political position of the second Truman Administration within the United States in order to better understand this apparent inconsistency.

Although Harry Truman had won an astounding victory against overwhelming odds in the national elections of November 1948, criticism of his foreign policy within his own party as well as among the Republicans continued to mount after the election was over. Before World War II the Republican

Below: MacArthur and George C Marshall were adversaries both during the war and after it. As Secretary of State Marshall feared MacArthur's quasi-independence in Japan.

Party had been largely an isolationist party. Most of its members consistently opposed American entry into World War II until Pearl Harbor, after which they loyally supported the American war effort. The general attitude in the United States after the war was that 'the boys should be brought back home' as soon as possible. America underwent one of the most dramatic demobilizations in modern history, reducing the armed forces to a tiny faction of their wartime peak of something over 15,000,000 under arms. At the same time Truman maintained an increasingly belligerent stance toward the Soviet Union and Communism in general. The USSR did not demobilize nearly as quickly or thoroughly as the Americans had done,

but the Soviets were war-weary, their country having been ravaged by the German army and their economy stretched to breaking point by the end of the war. Despite this, Stalin hoped to consolidate his hold over Eastern Europe, and established puppet governments in the states behind what Churchill had called the Iron Curtain.

The fall of China in 1949 was often attributed by Truman's critics to be yet another step in a Soviet bid for world hegemony, the assumption being that the Communist threat was monolithic under the direct control of Stalin. In the case of China there is no doubt whatever today that this assumption was false. Yet to an American public familiar with the failure of the appeasement policy in the

face of German, Italian and Japanese aggression before World War II, the failure to act decisively against what seemed to be a similar threat to world security by the USSR could be laid at the feet of Truman.

By 1949 the attacks by Senator Joseph R McCarthy of Wisconsin against the Democrats were beginning to attract a good deal of publicity. McCarthy, an

Left: The crew of a 40-mm gun watch as a salvo is fired by the battleship USS *Missouri* on the Chongjin area in North Korea in October 1950.
Below: Men of the 52nd Field Artillery fire on North Korean forces in the area above Angang-ni in September 1950. The combined might of the Allied powers was brought to bear on the Koreans, forcing Communist China into the conflict.

arch anti-Communist and demagogue, believed that there was some sort of conspiracy against American interests, of which he alleged the Democrats and Truman in particular to be a part. The Republican Party, under the leadership of moderates like Senator Arthur Vandenberg of Michigan and fanatics like McCarthy, soon became the party of intervention in Europe, advocating an American military build up to prevent her wartime allies, as well as the conquered states of Germany, Italy and Japan, from falling under the hand of Communism. Unsubstantiated charges of corruption and subversion within the Truman Administration were alleged by McCarthy as well as by some of his more respectable colleagues, and the trial and conviction of certain Russian spies, like Julius and Ethel Rosenberg, seemed to lend some weight to these charges. The trial of Alger Hiss became another focal point for attacks on Truman's loyalty to American national interests.

The charge that the Truman Administration was 'soft on Communism' is even more ludicrous in the light of historical hindsight. Although Truman was not quick to recognize a threat of subversion to some Western European governments, once roused he did act briskly and, at times, impetuously. Goaded on by the American right wing, he authorized General Marshall to make his famous speech at the Harvard Commencement of 1947 which inaugurated the Marshall Plan to help rebuild crumbling European economies.

The North Atlantic Treaty Organization, built on the Brussels Pact of 1948, was constructed throughout the election year and was formally launched a year later. Funding a military presence in Western Europe was not as quickly approved. Despite all these positive steps to stem the Communist tide, Truman was still urged to do more by the Republicans and he and Roosevelt were continually blamed for the 'sell-out' at Yalta, and the 'loss' of Czechoslovakia and China. Truman's courageous and even provocative action taken during the Berlin Blockade of 1948–49 was not given the credit it deserved. In the eyes of the opposition Truman could do nothing right, and he naturally felt a sense of frustration and resentment.

One of the heroes of the American right was MacArthur. His connections with right-wing elements in the Republican Party did not end with his failure at the Wisconsin primary. He continued to keep close liaison with Joe Martin, Republican Minority Leader in the House of Representatives. The Joint Chiefs were never known for their left-wing views, but in MacArthur's eyes a conspiracy between them and Truman as well as his urbane Secretary of State, Dean Acheson, was being concocted against him. MacArthur wanted to see American troops remain in Korea for two reasons: firstly, he believed that Communist aggression was likely to take place there, and secondly, he could exert control over Korea if troops were there. Without American troops, Korea was in the hands of the 'untrustworthy' State Department. How many more Alger Hisses were lurking there, McCarthy had charged, and MacArthur agreed.

MacArthur did not openly oppose the withdrawal of troops from Korea and he did echo the Pentagon's and State Department's sentiments that the American defense perimeter should not include Formosa or Korea. MacArthur was a friend to both aging dictators, Rhee of

Below: The Services Club in 1950. These institutions were set up at every US Army and Air Force installation after the war to supplement the work of the USO.

Korea and Chiang of Nationalist China (now just Formosa, the Pescadores and a few offshore islands). Although Chiang had a solid position on Formosa, thanks to his ruthless suppression of a native rebellion there in 1947, he could not maintain his independence from Mainland China for long without an American fleet to protect him from attack. Rhee, on the other hand, led a very shaky regime which was extremely unpopular. One reason why the Truman Administration kept South Korea out of the American defense perimeter was the fact that Rhee's ability to survive was more than uncertain. Although Washington had reaffirmed its intention to stay out of what it called 'the civil conflict in China' as late as 5 January 1950, it became increasingly clear that pressure on the government was mounting to 'do something' to stop the Communists.

In May 1950 Senator Tom Connally, Chairman of the Senate Foreign Relations Committee said in an interview, 'We've got to battle some time, why not now?' MacArthur indicated in his memoirs that he warned the Pentagon that an attack against South Korea was likely, and in one report indicated a probable time as June 1950. Collaboration between MacArthur and Rhee was a possibility. On 30 May, less than a month before the invasion took place, Rhee was decisively beaten in the South Korean

elections. Both Rhee and his Defense Ministry had warned in the waning days of the campaign that it was their intention to invade North Korea and could 'take Pyongyang in a few days.' One reason why the US had given South Korea only light weapons was to prevent Rhee from contemplating just such an action. Rhee was a man after MacArthur's own heart. MacArthur wanted to see Rhee strengthened as well as his own influence in Korea expanded. How was this to be done? If, however, South Korea would allow itself to stand as a sitting target, and if North Korea could be provoked into aggression against the south, Washington would be faced with a dilemma. The US could either rescind its stated policy toward Korea and allow the South to fall to the Communists, which would certainly have turned American public opinion against Truman and the Democrats; or it could help Rhee repel the aggressor, thereby strengthening Rhee's position in South Korea, and bring in American troops from Japan under MacArthur's command to intervene on Rhee's behalf. In either case MacArthur and those in the

United States who supported his viewpoint would benefit.

If Korea was allowed to fall with American troops in the vicinity, MacArthur could launch yet another presidential campaign on the charge that Truman had let another little country 'go down the drain' and that he could have stopped the Communists if Truman had let him. If, however, Truman authorized American resistance to such an invasion, and MacArthur led it, he would once again emerge as a war hero who had been right all along. Neither MacArthur, nor Truman, nor Acheson admit in their memoirs that MacArthur was thinking along these lines but there is some evidence to show that the invasion of South Korea was not entirely a surprise to him. He himself admits that he warned that it was quite possible, and Willoughby has stated that MacArthur's intelligence team was fully aware three months before the attack that a large military build up was taking place north of the 38th Parallel. Therefore, it is not entirely surprising that John Foster Dulles, a prominent member of the Republican Party and later Secretary of State under Eisenhower, reversed the stand of the US toward Korea when he visited the 38th Parallel less than a month before the attack. Collusion between Dulles and MacArthur is not out of the question.

Above: MacArthur meets with Madame Chiang Kai-shek in mid-1950. Madame Chiang was a most assidious worker in the Chinese Nationalist cause.

MacArthur states in his memoirs that Washington was naive when it did not encourage Syngman Rhee to unify the whole of Korea by force prior to 1950. Some American military advisors to Rhee's government welcomed the prospect of an attack by the North in order to test the Republic of Korea army (ROK) which they had been training, among them Brigadier General William L Roberts, chief of the military mission who told as much to American reporters in May 1950. Even when the first reports of an attack in Korea began to trickle in, the UN Temporary Commission on Korea thought that the attack was made on the North by South Korea rather than the other way around. Whatever the origins of the Korean conflict, a stunned world woke up to the news that North Korean regular army troops had crossed the 38th Parallel at about 0400 hours on 25 June 1950. It was a Sunday and many officers, including all but one of the Americans assigned to forward ROK units, were on leave. As a heavy rain fell North Korean units moved southward, plunging toward their first objective, Seoul, the capital of South Korea.

Left: Troops of the 5th Republic of Korea Division advance to join an attack on Communist positions in the Hamnhung area. They are to support an airborne unit of the US X Corps. The picture was taken in February 1951.

Far left: MacArthur and President Truman pictured during the Wake Island conference on 15 October 1951. Although the meeting was conducted in a cordial atmosphere it did not really improve relations between the two. MacArthur argued at the conference that the Chinese Communists would not intervene in the war in Korea.

Below: Infantry men of the 27th Regiment in well-prepared trenches near the Heartbreak Ridge position in August 1952. By that time the fighting had reached stalemate.

Above: MacArthur and his party inspect a beach during the landings by Australian troops on Balikpapan in Dutch Borneo. Australian forces were instrumental in helping the Allies secure both New Guinea and the Dutch East Indies.

Left: MacArthur signs the instrument of surrender of Japanese forces aboard the USS *Missouri* watched by the gaunt figures of Generals Percival and Wainwright, both of whom spent years in Japanese prison camps after the fall of Singapore and Corregidor respectively.

Right: Men of the X Corps in pursuit of the North Koreans and Chinese near Wonju in February 1951.

Below: MacArthur watches with other high ranking officers including General Edward Almond (right) as the Marines land at Inchon on 15 September 1950. The group observed from the USS *Mount McKinley*.

Below right: Members of the 1st Battalion, 187th Airborne RCT clean their weapons during a lull in the fighting along a stabilized line in February 1951.

Above: Painting of the Inchon invasion, MacArthur's most daring military exploit, which proved to be the capstone to his already illustrious military career.

Above: Anti-Communist poster issued by the ROK Army portraying the North Koreans as pawns or marionettes in the hands of the Russian bear.

Below: A wounded soldier is evacuated to the 1st Mobile Army Surgical Hospital (MASH) in Chechon, Korea in March 1951.

Below: Men of the 24th Infantry Division
in a foxhole on the perimeter of the area
of defense near Hwachon in 1951.

Bottom: Artillerymen of the US 8th Army
cover their ears as their 8-inch howitzer
fires a salvo at Communist-held Hill 983.

Above: A painting of General of the Army
Douglas MacArthur by Thomas E
Stephens in 1950.

Right: Soldiers of the 25th Division guard the UN encampment at Munsan-ni in Korea in 1951. The war continued for two fruitless years after MacArthur was recalled with battle lines at the ceasefire roughly what they were over two years before.

Below: Public viewing of the body of General Douglas MacArthur lying in the Rotunda of the MacArthur Memorial Building in Norfolk, Virginia on 11 April 1964 exactly thirteen years after his recall from Korea and Japan.

6: THE WARRIOR UNLEASHED

President Truman was at home on Saturday evening, 24 June 1950, spending the weekend with his family in Independence, Missouri. Secretary of State Acheson told him on the telephone 'Mr President, I have some very serious news. The North Koreans have invaded South Korea.' Acheson advised the President that the US should call upon the Security Council of the UN to meet at once and ask them to declare that an act of aggression had taken place. The following morning, shortly before the Trumans sat down to Sunday dinner, Acheson called again. He said there was no doubt that a full-scale invasion had been launched, and he added that the UN was likely to call for a ceasefire, which would probably be ignored. The United States would have to make an immediate decision as to the degree of support, if any, it was prepared to give to the government of Syngman Rhee. Truman asked Acheson to arrange an immediate meeting with the Joint Chiefs of Staff and told him he was returning to Washington at once. Within an hour he was in the air and in three more he was in Washington.

Like many other Americans, Truman felt that the situation in Korea was comparable to the Japanese invasion of Manchuria in 1931, or Hitler's 1938 *Anschluss* with Austria. The dictators were not stopped then, and what was the result? They had to be fought later under less favorable conditions. Truman truly believed that to allow this incident to go unnoticed would encourage the Communists to go on and on, and would, in fact, lead the world toward a third war. The Joint Chiefs, Acheson and other State Department officials, including Deputy Under Secretary Dean Rusk and Ambassador-at-Large Philip Jessup talked over dinner in the White House, and afterward, the State and Defense Departments presented their joint re-

Left: Ground troops of the 3rd ROK Division march past the Diamond Mountains on their northward drive toward Wonsan in North Korea early in October 1950.

commendations to be acted upon immediately. MacArthur was to be ordered to evacuate Americans from Korea, including all dependents, but he should try to keep the key airports in Korea open. Therefore, his air forces were to remain south of the 38th Parallel. He was also to get ammunition and supplies to the South Koreans by air drop and other means. The American Seventh Fleet in the Pacific should be sent to the Formosa Strait to prevent action in that area; in other words, to prevent Chiang from attacking mainland China and/or to protect Formosa against possible invasion from the mainland. American policy had now altered; Formosa and Korea were to be included in a new American defense perimeter. These instructions were telephoned to MacArthur at once.

MacArthur's feelings at the time of the attack were not too dissimilar from those of Truman. He heard the news of the attack in his bedroom at the American Embassy in Tokyo in the early hours of Sunday morning. To MacArthur, as he describes it, it was like a nightmare, a repetition of 7 December 1941. He quickly moved to evacuate the Americans from Korea after orders were received from Washington, but apart from sending planes to accomplish this operation, he did nothing else at first. Soon orders to resist Communist aggression and to commit American troops to the field were received and acted upon. One can only imagine MacArthur's true feelings at this time. After a successful military career in World War II, after a successful administration of postwar Japan which was not yet completed, an occupation which even his enemies praised, MacArthur had probably no more than an honored retirement to look forward to. Now events had given him a new role: as commander of US forces in Korea (and subsequently UN forces) he had a chance at glory and fame once more. Undaunted and thrilled by the challenge, MacArthur prepared his staff for what was to be his last campaign.

Meanwhile, in New York, the UN Security Council was quickly called into session. On the 27th (US Eastern Daylight Time), after two special sessions, the UN agreed to ask North Korea to halt its activities and withdraw behind the 38th Parallel. When this request was denied, it then recommended member states to 'furnish such assistance to the Republic of Korea as may be necessary to repel the armed attack.' Even before the UN asked its members to help South Korea the US had done so of its own accord. Truman chose to interpret the first UN directive, which was far more vague than its explicit instructions of the 27th, as an authorization to help South Korea unilaterally. With or without the UN approval the US would have acted. UN approval was almost a certainty, however. The Soviet Union, a permanent member of the Security Council with veto power, had absented herself for several months prior to the beginning of the Korean War in protest against the UN's refusal to seat Communist China in place of the Nationalist government in the General Assembly and Security Council. In Soviet absence a vote of

seven to one was possible, with Egypt and India abstaining and Yugoslavia voting against UN action.

An hour after the Security Council vote was taken Truman ordered MacArthur to give the Korean government troops cover and support from American naval and air forces. The following day, the 28th, Britain placed its armed forces in the area at the disposal of MacArthur. Therefore, from the very start, bar the first anxious hours of the war, the American intervention on South Korea's behalf was not unilateral; it was decided upon under the aegis of the United Nations with the help of allies, many of which were to follow Britain's lead. Hesitatingly America went to war. But it was a war by some other name. Sometimes called the Korean 'conflict,' later dubbed a 'police action,' American troops were committed to an undeclared war, a constitutional fine point overlooked until later on. MacArthur had hoped that the United States would formally declare war against North Korea, but this constitutional step was never taken.

Truman feared that a formal declaration of war might hasten the possible entry of the Soviet Union and/or China into the war, or that the whole affair,

with or without a declaration, might encourage a Soviet attack elsewhere – in the Middle East or Berlin – as a countermeasure.

MacArthur saw the conflict in more clear-cut terms. War was waged to be won. Even at the beginning every bit of previous training MacArthur had enjoyed – at West Point, in both world wars – had pointed to a policy of victory. Limited war, of the sort that Truman envisaged, was not acceptable in MacArthur's terms. A military man to his fingertips, MacArthur believed in the Clausewitzian approach; if war was an extension of diplomacy, if it were to be used as a last resort, then it should be waged wholeheartedly. This attitude he took into the conflict, and it suited his political ends. For if Truman limited MacArthur's sphere of action, as was apparent from the beginning, MacArthur and his Republican allies at home could use this forced restraint as a stick with which to beat the Democrats. MacArthur, furthermore, could not achieve the sort of heroism he enjoyed in World War II if his hands were tied. Thus, he was emotionally and politically ill-equipped to carry out Truman's orders; that is, to prevent the fall of South Korea without any reference to an attempt to help Syngman Rhee conquer the whole of the peninsula for the Republic of Korea. Reunification of Korea was to be prevented, not encouraged, whether by the South or North Koreans.

In those first days of the war MacArthur had few thoughts about a push northward. He doubted if the few American troops that could be spared from their base in Japan and Okinawa would be sufficient to stem the Communist tide. By the time Truman fully committed the US to take action, North Korean troops were in the suburbs of the South Korean capital, Seoul. On 29 June MacArthur flew over to take a look. Seoul had fallen on the 28th and the situation was becoming increasingly desperate. MacArthur was reporting ROK casualties of up to 50 percent to the Pentagon before his plane, the *Bataan*, a Constellation, took off for Korea. The South Korean government had fled to Taejon, and MacArthur landed 20 miles south of Seoul to watch the city go up in flames which were visible across the Han River. Thousands of discouraged and disorganized ROK troops passed him.

Below: The Wonsan Oil Refinery under attack by aircraft of the US Seventh Fleet soon after the invasion of South Korea in early July 1950.

Above: Weary artillerymen rest in the rain during the long retreat to the Pusan Perimeter in late July 1950. UN Forces were almost pushed into the sea.

MacArthur expressed confidence that he could hold the North Koreans at the Han, but privately his thoughts flashed back to Bataan and Corregidor, when the flight of Filipinos spelled doom for Manila and ultimately the American and Philippine troops who were trapped once the capital had fallen. Without US troops the Republic of Korea was finished. The American training which the ROKs had received had already proved woefully inadequate.

While MacArthur was in Korea Truman announced to the press that 'we are not at war,' but he was made aware that his commitment of naval and air forces to the Republic would not be enough to stop the Communists. As days passed it also became apparent to Truman that US and UN intervention was not provoking Russia or China to take immediate countermeasures, and his will strengthened. On 30 June MacArthur asked Truman to allow him to send a Regimental Combat Team to Korea as a first step in an American ground commitment. Truman authorized this at once, having been besieged by South Korean delegates in Washington who

pleaded to Truman, begging for massive military assistance. It was at this point that Chiang Kai-shek offered troops for the Korean War. Truman recognized that the entry of Nationalist Chinese troops would trigger an entry of Communist China into the war. Furthermore, without sufficient military hardware Chiang's troops would suffer the same fate as that now being suffered by the ROKs. Truman later wrote that it was at this juncture that he decided to authorize MacArthur to use the ground troops under his command, which meant all four divisions of the Eighth Army in Japan, or whatever MacArthur could spare. At Admiral Sherman's suggestion a naval blockade of the entire Korean coast was ordered. All these instructions were sent forward on 30 June. The following day the first two companies of the 24th Infantry Division arrived at Pusan, on the southern tip of Korea, and then pushed northward to engage the North Koreans. America and, by implication, the UN was now fully committed to defend the South.

MacArthur was to need all the help he could get. On the 29th the Australians informed Acheson that their naval vessels and small fighter squadron in the area could be placed at MacArthur's disposal, and two days later they were in the field, the first non-American units to go into

action. MacArthur realized that a long retreat would have to be followed by a stabilization of a line somewhere in front of Pusan, the South's major port, and plans were already being made for a counterattack. As the war progressed and as the South Koreans withdrew, MacArthur's authority solidified; the American containment policy, of which the Marshall Plan, NATO and Berlin Blockade had been a part, was endorsed further by the United Nations when, on 7 July, the Security Council completely identified its aims with those of the United States. The UN flag could be used along with the flags of the participating nations in Korea, and the following day MacArthur was given a new title by Truman: Commander in Chief of the Unified Command, the United Nations Command (CINCUNC) to add to his title of CINCFE (C in C Far East), a purely American designation. His GHQ became General Headquarters, United Nations Command (GHQ UNC). MacArthur continued to see himself as the agent of the United States responsible only to the President, who was the agent of the UN. It was a fine point but a crucial one, as events proved.

The day he received his new title MacArthur asked for more men. The Eighth Army was understrength as it was, and now that he was committing it

to the field in Korea he needed replacements to continue his occupation of Japan. He asked for no less than five more divisions and three tank battalions to enable him 'by amphibious maneuver' to strike behind North Korean lines. The Joint Chiefs vetoed his request. The reasons given were that no increase in any part of the armed services had been authorized; there was a shortage of adequate shipping; and that forces in other areas (Germany and Western

Above: Soldier of the 25th Infantry Division throws a grenade at a North Korean sniper, hiding in a village 20 miles north of Taegu in late August, 1950.

Europe primarily) had to be maintained. MacArthur was again faced, as he had been throughout World War II, with the fact that American strategic interests differed from his own: Europe first as opposed to Asia first. He was infuriated. At least in 1942 there was a war going on in Europe. The refusal to send more troops seemed incomprehensible, and he felt let down badly by his government. He decided in the interim to bring American units in Korea to full strength

Below: Private of the 25th Infantry Division in action in the Taegu area uses his .30 caliber machine gun against North Korean forces pressing on the Pusan Perimeter.

by adding South Korean troops, and he persuaded the Yoshida government in Japan to form a 'national police reserve' and coast guard units, almost 100,000 men in all. Thus the onset of the Korean War was the first step in Japan's abandonment of her pledge never to rearm. Meanwhile, MacArthur's sea and air forces quickly mastered the air above and the seas around Korea. South Korean troops, thanks to the initial help given by the Americans, held the Han River Line, which the North did not cross until 3 July. Then they began to fall back. Reinforcements were landed at Pusan under the command of Major General William F Dean, and the Eighth Army under Lieutenant General Walton H Walker was given direct responsibility for the Korean campaign.

The Americans had an exceedingly rough time in the first weeks of their intervention in Korea. Over half the men of the first two companies deployed were lost after having been attacked by more than 30 tanks and two infantry regiments. Dean's reinforcements, however, were able to hold the line 25 miles further south, but only after a heavy number of casualties. MacArthur informed General Walker that Rhee had asked him to place the ROK troops under his command, so from 20 July onward the major tactical decisions were in Walker's hands.

Meanwhile, MacArthur's political offensive in the US was gathering steam. He had already gained the whole-hearted support of the press and radio and then went on to publish a statement indicating that far more help was needed in Korea if the breach was to be adequately filled, admitting at the same time that casualties were running at a very high rate. He urged that 'the situation has developed into a major operation.' The following day the 2nd Division and other stateside units were ordered to go to Japan. Now that the Americans were deeply committed to the Korean intervention, MacArthur flew to Formosa to confer with Chiang Kai-shek, bringing Willoughby, Almond, Stratemeyer and Whitney with him, but excluding his senior diplomatic officer, Sebald. This meeting with the Generalissimo met with stout criticism

Left: Pershing M-26 tanks, which were developed into the more sophisticated M-46 tanks, fire at an observation post across the Naktong River in August, 1950.

Above: President Syngman Rhee of the Republic of Korea and MacArthur salute the colors as the General prepares to return to Korea from Haneda Airbase, Tokyo.

in Washington, despite the fact that the Joint Chiefs had been aware of the mission and had, albeit reluctantly, approved it.

Truman wanted no wider war, and he feared collusion between Chiang and MacArthur to somehow bring Nationalist China into the war despite Truman's strict orders that they were to be kept out. Truman disliked Chiang. He reputedly was planning to drop his recognition of the Nationalist regime shortly before the war and give diplomatic recognition to Mao's government, but the war prevented this from taking place. The President was concerned enough about the Chiang-MacArthur meeting to send his personal diplomatic representative, Averell Harriman, to restate American policy toward Chiang. Before his arrival in Tokyo MacArthur repeated his praise of the Generalissimo and his 'determination to resist Communist domination.' Harriman brought General Lawrence Norstad and General Matthew B Ridg-

way, the Deputy Chief of Staff, with him to Tokyo. Only they and General Almond were present when MacArthur presented his plan for victory in Korea. He felt that an offensive had to be launched before winter set in, otherwise it would be too late. Delay, MacArthur felt, would only encourage an eventual Chinese or Soviet intervention. He also stated that if China launched an attack on Formosa he would assume command and 'deliver such a crushing defeat it would be one of the decisive battles of the world – a disaster so great it would rock Asia and perhaps turn back Communism.' He admitted that he prayed nightly that such an attack would take place.

Harriman left MacArthur with the opinion that although he was loyal to 'constitutional authority,' he had 'a strange idea that we should back anybody who will fight Communism.' This was a fair assessment of MacArthur's viewpoint, which he underlined in a speech which he sent to the Veterans of Foreign Wars (VFW) which was to be read to their annual convocation. As usual in such cases, the address had to be vetted by the Pentagon. Truman asked that the

message be withdrawn because of its variance with American policy. Among other things MacArthur stated in this speech that 'nothing could be more fallacious than the threadbare argument by those who advocate appeasement and defeatism in the Pacific that if we defend Formosa we alienate continental Asia. Those who speak thus do not understand the Orient.' The message was formally withdrawn, but it had already been printed in advance in the house journal of the VFW. This was a highly provocative act by a soldier in the field against his commanding officer, the President. It was, of course, meant to enrage right-wing opinion in America against the President and it had the desired effect. Behind MacArthur's reasoning was a long-felt distrust for the British who were working in close harmony with the President. He mistrusted particularly the Attlee government and even believed that the State Department, under the leadership of the dapper Dean Acheson whose cultured accent sounded British to most American ears, was under the influence of Whitehall.

MacArthur honestly believed that the American government was, at best, misguided and misinformed about Asia, and at worst, subverted by socialists, crypto-Communists and Anglophiles. He was now set on his collision course with the Truman Administration. Truman already was considering his replacement as SCAP and CINCFE by Omar Bradley, whose political interests were minimal and whose military competence was already proven. Truman claims in his memoirs that he did not want to hurt MacArthur personally by demoting him. Closer to the truth might be the assumption that the relief of MacArthur would be politically disastrous for the Democrats in 1950, an election year for the House and Senate. If MacArthur were fired the Democrats would certainly once more lose control of both Houses as they had done in 1946, thereby putting a stop to the Fair Deal program of domestic legislation that Truman wanted to see through. Therefore he held his hand from this dramatic step, but waited for another opportunity. In the meantime, he sent MacArthur a personal message underlining the government's stance vis-à-vis Formosa and Korea.

Although there was a political stalemate now between MacArthur and the Truman Administration, there was hardly a stalemate in Korea. South Korean and American forces in the field were being systematically chewed up by the North Korean offensive, and units were being pulled back into the Pusan Perimeter, a semi-circular enclave in the southeast corner of the peninsula, where MacArthur intended to hold the line until a counteroffensive could be launched. MacArthur's mind was set on a landing behind North Korean lines in a manner similar to the amphibious landings that had led him from Papua to the Philippines. MacArthur's remaining force, the 7th Division, was to be held back for a surprise attack, while the rest of his units were deployed around the periphery of the Pusan Perimeter. The Eighth Army held the left flank, a dangerous sector stretching some 65 miles, with three divisions in the line – the 25th, 24th and 1st Cavalry. The I and II South Korean Corps would hold the right flank with their five divisions. MacArthur believed that 'self-preservation' would induce the men to fight to the last to hold the perimeter, for if it fell there was insufficient naval support to evacuate them all to Japan. Mac-

Arthur's mind was firmly set on a landing at Inchon, well to the north, which, if successful, would trap the North Koreans behind their extended supply lines and force a massive withdrawal from the South. By the end of August, when the UN's back was to the wall, he appointed General Almond to lead X Corps to conduct this operation. The Corps was to be built from the 7th Division and the 1st Marine Division.

The Joint Chiefs had approved an amphibious landing from the moment it had been suggested. Its advantage lay in MacArthur's virtually unchallenged naval and air superiority. But they were not so enthusiastic about MacArthur's choice of a landing place. Inchon was far to the north, near Seoul where there would inevitably be a tough fight, and Inchon's high tides would make landing difficult. Inchon would leave no room for failure. If the landings were repelled

Below: MacArthur and *Life* photographer and *New York Herald Tribune* correspondent Marguerite Higgins, who was the most outstanding reporter to record the war.

most of the men would be lost. Mac-Arthur, however, had enormous confidence in his own military judgment, which most of his colleagues in Japan and Washington shared. At a conference held in Tokyo on 23 July the objections were raised and the Army Chief of Staff, J Lawton Collins, and the Chief of Naval Operations, Admiral Forrest P Sherman, who were flown out from Washington for the occasion, suggested that the landings take place further south at Kunsan. MacArthur answered these objections with his usual eloquence and incisiveness. He felt that a landing at Kunsan would not successfully cut the North Koreans' communications, whereas a success at Inchon would almost certainly guarantee that as well as the fall of Seoul, which would have enormous political and military implications. Inchon was not prepared for defense. Most of the North Korean army was surrounding the Pusan Perimeter. MacArthur likened an attack at Inchon to the surprise Wolfe had enjoyed at

Below: The main map portrays the invasion at Inchon on 15 September, 1950, and the inset indicates the subsequent encirclement of Seoul, completed two weeks after the landings.

Quebec. In that action in 1759, the forces of Montcalm were taken totally by surprise and never recovered the initiative in the Battle of the Plains of Abraham. He concluded with a peroration, asserting that if Communism was stopped in its tracks in Asia world peace would be secured. But if it were not, the fate of Europe would be in danger. 'I can almost hear the ticking of the second hand of destiny.' The premise was shaky but it convinced his audience. Although Collins remained doubtful, the others were convinced. The landings were to take place at Inchon.

The Joint Chiefs finally agreed to MacArthur's plan on 29 August; by then the Pusan Perimeter was under intense attack. So was Truman. In the Senate Taft and Knowland were asserting that Formosa should be defended at all costs and that subversion in the State Department was weakening the resolve of the United States to fight Communism. Far Eastern specialists like John Stewart Service, Owen Lattimore and Philip Jessup were being charged with having been 'soft on Communism' for having considered Chairman Mao to have been merely an agrarian reformer, not a total revolutionary as the Republicans be-

lieved him to be. Even after the decision had been made to go ahead at Inchon, MacArthur received a query from the Joint Chiefs about the feasibility of the plan. Someone was getting cold feet. Was it the President? Marshall, who had just been appointed Secretary of Defense? Bradley? Or was it something more sinister? In any event MacArthur replied that he gave the Inchon plan every chance of success, and received another go-ahead on the strength of his reply. The President concurred and Inchon was to be launched according to the existing plan.

On 15 September, the designated day of the Inchon landing, the morning high tide would be at 0659 hours and the evening tide at 1919. The tides in the channels leading to Inchon had a range of over 30 feet. A tide of 23 feet was necessary to allow the LSTs to navigate their way to the narrow peninsula where the landings were to take place. There would be no room for error or delay. The boats had to land and depart within the specified time or be stranded helplessly on the sand bar, exposed to any North Korean counterattack. In short, it had to be perfect. Faint hearts faltered when a typhoon hit Kobe on 3 September just

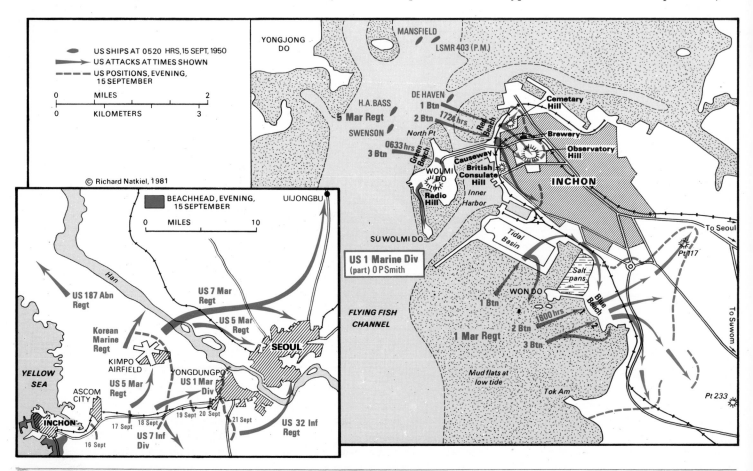

Above: Marines scale the ladders to disembark at Inchon in the most daring amphibious invasion ever mounted. It was MacArthur's greatest triumph.

as the 1st Marine Division, which Walker pleaded for to bolster his sagging defenses in the Pusan Perimeter, was embarking. This stroke of bad luck interrupted the loading and damaged some of the vessels and equipment. 'Operation Chromite,' as the landings were designated, was set in motion, despite the fact that a second typhoon was detected moving toward Korea and due to arrive somewhere around the 12th or 13th. An armada of some 260 ships set out from Japan on 5th September, carrying nearly 70,000 men. It included vessels from Australia, Canada, New Zealand, France and the Netherlands, as well as the British light carrier, *Triumph*. All movements were on schedule when the typhoon Kezia zeroed in with winds of up to 125 mph on 11 September. It was considered one of the worst storms any of the men had encountered. The ships were ordered to hold their course if the whole operation was not to be dislocated, but luckily Kezia

drifted away from the invasion force. MacArthur, Almond and Whitney flew down from Tokyo to Itazuke on the 12th and boarded the flagship *Mount McKinley* at Saebo to set out for Inchon in the early hours of the next morning. It was the anniversary of Quebec. By the time the *Mount McKinley* arrived off Inchon on the 14th the coast had been heavily bombarded for five days. The heaviest bombardment was reserved for Wolmi-do, an island off the Inchon coast, where one of the three landings was to take place. Wolmi-do was connected to the mainland by a thin causeway. The idea was that if the landing on the mainland went wrong, the Allies could defend Wolmi-do for a time until reinforcements arrived. But it was very tricky nevertheless. Everything depended on the taking of Wolmi-do swiftly.

On D-Day, 15 September, the first troops of the 5th Marines began to land at Green Beach, Wolmi-do, at 0633 hours. They were greeted only by scattered shots in the lightly-defended area. The flag was raised on Radio Hill, which dominated Inchon harbor, at 0655. The whole of this 105-meter high feature which had caused the Pentagon

so much worry was taken by 0800 hours. MacArthur had seen the flag go up from his position on the bridge of the *Mount McKinley*. He sent a message to Vice-Admiral Struble aboard his flagship *Rochester*: 'The navy and the marines have never shone more brightly than this morning, MacArthur.' Wolmi-do had been taken without a single fatality as well as the islet attached to it, Suwolmi-do, where the defenders, although dazed by the surprise attack, fought hard. There had been only about 350 defenders of Wolmi-do. The naval and air bombardment continued all day, but the second wave had to wait for the evening tide. The main landings took place at 1730 as the tide flowed in. The landings at Red Beach were not as easy as those at Green, and there was a tough fight for Cemetery Hill in Inchon itself where a North Korean bunker pinned down the Marines below a sea wall. By midnight a firm line across Observatory Hill which controlled Red Beach was held. The Red Beach assault had meant that within six hours the Marines were firmly placed inside the city of Inchon. Everything had gone almost exactly according to plan. At Blue Beach, the mainland

Above: MacArthur and Brigadier General Courtney Whitney observe the shelling of Inchon from the USS *Mount McKinley*, the day of the invasion, 15 September 1950.

landing, some craft were grounded in mud 300 feet offshore and the Marines were forced to wade ashore. Some vehicles were stalled when a road collapsed, but after a sea wall was dynamited, the landings on Blue Beach went more smoothly. By midnight even the attackers from Blue Beach had reached their objectives, and by morning the following day the North Koreans had been driven from Inchon. The first part of the victory had been won cheaply. There were only 196 casualties and of these only about 20 killed in action. MacArthur's courage and judgment had been justified. The American public awoke to learn of an astonishing victory snatched from the jaws of what has seemed to be a desperate situation. MacArthur's stock with the American people was never higher.

The initial victory had to be followed by a swift advance toward Kimpo airfield and Seoul itself. The North Korean High Command had written off Inchon and intended to make a stand at Seoul, which was now turned into a fortress. As the rest of the landing force disembarked MacArthur landed with Struble, Almond and the others and visited the

battlefield. He predicted that the UN forces would take Seoul within five days; it turned out to be almost two weeks as Almond had predicted. The North Koreans defended the capital fiercely, and by the time they evacuated Seoul on the 28th 130,000 prisoners had been taken. The next day MacArthur went to Kimpo airfield and at midday, at a ceremony held in the hall of the South Korean National Assembly MacArthur dramatically proclaimed the city of Seoul restored as the seat of government. Rhee was asked to resume his 'discharge of the civil responsibility.' With tears flowing down his cheeks Rhee replied on behalf of his people, 'We admire you. We love you as the savior of our race.' MacArthur flew back to Tokyo that afternoon, having recorded his greatest triumph in his long and glorious military career.

The question now was whether and to what extent to pursue the enemy. Washington was worried about Russian or Chinese intervention if American forces crossed the 38th Parallel. The fact that technically this was a UN force would not worry the Communists much; there were only token UN contingents. This was massively an American and South Korean show. Truman came to the conclusion that North Korean forces had to be destroyed, and to give them privileged sanctuary north of the Parallel would

make it difficult if not impossible for the war to be successfully and quickly concluded. MacArthur felt that the placing of the Seventh Fleet in the Formosa Strait allowed Mao to release at least 500,000 men for possible duty in Korea. From a military standpoint this was correct. There is little likelihood that Chiang would have crossed the Strait and invaded China without American support, and although MacArthur was in charge of the entire Western Pacific area, Washington could always deny him sufficient forces to carry on a two-front war in China/Formosa and Korea, knowing that MacArthur would not launch any offensive unless there was a reasonable chance for military success.

As MacArthur pointed out, there always remained the chance that China would intervene in the war with or without reference to the Formosa question. Therefore, MacArthur's criticism of Truman on the question of the Seventh Fleet was well-founded. Of course, no one in Washington wanted a general war. MacArthur himself would not have welcomed Chinese intervention *per se*. But when the fateful decision was sent to MacArthur on 27 September by

Right: Admiral Arthur Radford, CINCPAC, MacArthur, Secretary of the Army Frank Pace and General Omar Bradley confer during the Wake Island conference on 15 October 1950.

Left: MacArthur and Major General M Almond stop at a command post of the 1st Marine Division on the road to Seoul on 20 September 1950.

the Joint Chiefs authorizing his forces to cross the 38th Parallel, a dramatic change took place in the Korean War. It was no longer to be, as the UN had ordered, a war to defend South Korea against aggression; it was now a war whose ultimate aim was the unification of Korea under the government of Syngman Rhee. The success of this operation would leave an American ally, perhaps even an American puppet regime, on the borders of China and Russia. Even the most sanguine observer of this event would recognize the monumental importance of this step.

The order from the Pentagon, however, was not clear-cut. Although a military objective was stated – namely the destruction of the North Korean

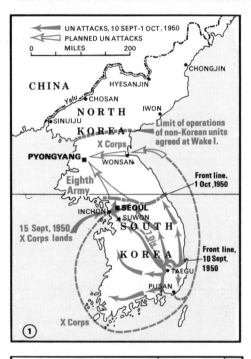

Above: MacArthur watches from the window of his plane as paratroops are dropped behind the lines of the North Koreans, as the UN Forces press toward the Yalu River in late October 1950.
Right: Men and tanks of the 7th Infantry Division advance toward the Yalu River in November 1950. The 7th was the first Allied force to reach as far north as the Chinese border.
Left: The initial stages of the UN offensive after the Inchon operation and the breakout from the Pusan perimeter.
Below left: The advance to the Yalu and the Chinese counteroffensive.

army – no UN troops were to be used in the frontier area abutting on the Soviet Union or China. Under no circumstances, the order stated, were troops to cross these frontiers, and Soviet and Chinese air space was not to be violated. MacArthur further was forced to prepare no plans for operations north of the 38th Parallel without specific approval. MacArthur correctly objected to the constricting nature of his directive. On 30 September he submitted a plan to the Pentagon which was approved at once. MacArthur's plan was first to send the Eighth Army across the Parallel with the objective of seizing Pyongyang, the enemy capital. X Corps would effect an amphibious landing at Wonsan, making a juncture with the Eighth Army. ROK forces would operate north of the line Chungjo-Yongwon-Hungnam, and the attack would take place during the latter half of October. The approval of this plan indicates that any criticism of MacArthur for having crossed the 38th Parallel without proper authority was unfounded. MacArthur then asked to be given permission to state that the 38th Parallel should not be a factor in the deployment of UN forces.

The same day, 1 October, he asked the North Korean Commander in Chief for his surrender, which was not forthcoming, even though North Korean forces, hemmed in on two sides, were straggling back to regroup north of the Parallel despite the loss of many men, much of their equipment, and the taking of thousands of prisoners. Chou En-lai, speaking that same day in Peking, warned that China would not stand aside

if 'the imperialists' invaded North Korean territory. Even at this point MacArthur suspected that China had sent an uncertain number of 'volunteers' to bolster the defenses of Pyongyang. Despite the growing danger of a Chinese intervention, MacArthur continued to carry out his plan and on 6 October the General Assembly of the United Nations approved MacArthur's plan of attack in North Korea.

Nevertheless, Truman, distrusting MacArthur, felt it best to sort out his differences with him in person. He invited him to a meeting either at Honolulu or at Wake Island. Marshall, the Secretary of Defense, felt that MacArthur should be informed of Washington's overall strategy with respect to the containment of Communism, in particular the American government's desire to give the defense of Europe top priority and not risk a general war over issues involving Korea or the Far East. The nature of this meeting was more than simply the Commander in Chief asking his top general to confer with him. It was more in the nature of one head of state inviting another head of state to an international conference. After all, Washington is a good deal farther than Tokyo from either Honolulu or Wake, and since MacArthur chose Wake, in terms of protocol this implied that Truman was going most of the way to meet MacArthur in geographic terms. The fact that he was hoping to meet him more than halfway in the talks was implied as well. The meeting was set for 15 October. Meanwhile, a week before, the first units of Eighth Army crossed the 38th Parallel into North Korea.

Truman's plane stopped in California and then in Hawaii, arriving on Wake on the morning of 15 October.

MacArthur was naturally wary of the man he had heard was hot-tempered and quick to react, but in his memoirs he says that he found Truman engaging and witty and that he 'liked him from the start.' MacArthur said that Truman seemed to enjoy the laugh that followed. They talked alone for over an hour, and first discussed the situation in both Japan and Korea. According to Truman, MacArthur assured him that the war in Korea was won; he reported that in his judgment the Communists would not dare to attack the formidable UN military machine, since MacArthur's forces had largely unopposed domination of the air. MacArthur said later that he did not unequivocally state that the Chinese would not intervene; just that they were unlikely to do so despite the heavy concentrations of Chinese troops by the Yalu River, the border between Manchuria and Korea. Then MacArthur apologized for having made the controversial statement to the Veterans of Foreign Wars. Truman said that as far as he was concerned, the incident was closed. Their talks turned to a discussion of the American political scene. MacArthur asked Truman if he planned to run again for the Presidency in 1952. Truman answered by asking MacArthur if he had any ambitions along those lines. MacArthur replied, 'None whatsoever. If you have any general running against you, his name will be Eisenhower, not MacArthur.' Truman seemed to enjoy this. He told MacArthur that 'Eisenhower doesn't know the first thing about politics. Why, if he should become President, his Administration would make Grant's look like a model of perfection.'

Later in the day, after their private meeting was over, Truman gave MacArthur the chance to restate his position concerning a Soviet or Chinese intervention to the larger group. Truman

Above: GIs eat their Thanksgiving Dinner beside the Yalu in November 1950. MacArthur's hopes of ending the war then were dashed by the Chinese intervention.

reports that MacArthur felt this simply would not happen, as they would be chewed up by the UN air forces, and in any event, the USSR and China would not and could not cooperate even if China dealt with the war on the ground and the Soviets with the air war. But Truman suggested that if this were the case, it might be possible to transfer some units to Europe by the end of the year. MacArthur, naturally enough, fought this suggestion. Truman left for San Francisco the same day and MacArthur returned to Tokyo. Truman felt that the discussions had gone on well. He presented MacArthur with the Distinguished Service Medal at the airport; it was the fifth time that MacArthur had received this award.

In fact the conference had not gone

as well as either man pretended. First of all, although it had been agreed that no notes would be taken at the talks, both MacArthur and Truman had secretly arranged for secretaries to take down the minutes of the meeting. Neither man trusted the other. MacArthur, in consonance with American Intelligence in general, underestimated the Chinese threat. Not only did China dare to take on the UN, it had far more men to deploy than MacArthur had reckoned. MacArthur left with a feeling that Truman was not nearly the man Roosevelt had been, and Truman felt that he had clearly stated America's world position. Neither man really took serious note of the other's intentions. For Truman this was a last chance on MacArthur's part to 'be a good boy'; for MacArthur this was a courtesy call paid to him by a somewhat mediocre, if amiable man. MacArthur felt that the British, especially, and other members of the UN who were contributing forces

to the Korean effort were swaying Truman unduly from the path of American national interest. MacArthur perceived that interest to be a pushing back of Communism wherever possible, while Truman, in his effort to avoid a world war now that Russia possessed an atomic bomb capability, felt that a policy of peaceful coexistence with Communism was the only sane policy that the US could follow. As long as MacArthur kept to his plan there would be no cause for concern. Five days after the Wake Island conference the Eighth Army entered the North Korean capital of Pyongyang.

In October and November more Allied units arrived in Korea: Australian, Dutch, British, Thai, Canadian and Turkish. A 9th Division was formed and South Korean units incorporated into the Eighth Army were returned to the ROK forces. Waves of men and materiel were poured into Japan from the US to

Below: MacArthur confers with Major General John Coulter in North Korea. Standing in the jeep is Lieutenant-General Walton Walker who was killed soon afterward.

Left: Men of the 7th Marines are evacuated from Nungnam on 11 December 1950, after the Chinese entered the war. The Marines fought in the Chosin Reservoir area.

support the United Nations effort. Mac-Arthur felt he had enough. In accordance with the Wake Island agreement, plans were made to send the US 2nd Division home; troops and supplies being sent directly to Pusan were diverted to Japan or Hawaii. MacArthur even made plans for the Eighth Army to assist in the rehabilitation of Korea once the country was unified and the war over. 'Home by Christmas' became a slogan in American homes.

On the military front, however, Mac-Arthur made two moves which were to have subsequent significance. On 17 October, only two days after the Wake Island conference, he authorized American forces to advance to a line only 30 or 40 miles from the Manchurian frontier, well above the line he had fixed in his initial victory plan. On 24 October he lifted all restrictions on the movements of UN troops. The Joint Chiefs did nothing about this despite the fact that this was directly contrary to the orders they approved less than a month before. Meanwhile, the North Koreans were being routed. After the fall of Pyongyang and the successful amphibious operations of the X Corps at Wonsan, the 7th Division made an unopposed landing 150 miles to the north as the Allies pressed the attack. An airborne regiment was landed 30 miles north of Pyongyang to cut off the fleeing North Koreans' escape route, and MacArthur watched the operations from the air. MacArthur landed at Pyongyang and declared that the war was all but over, but he was concerned, as General Walker was, that his supply lines were becoming dangerously stretched. In the light of the ominous Chinese buildup north of the Yalu this implied that MacArthur's air forces needed bolstering up. MacArthur wanted to pursue enemy planes across the Yalu into Chinese territory and the Pentagon forbade it. On 5 November the Joint Chiefs learned that MacArthur had authorized the bombing of bridges across

Left: The UN forces were forced to evacuate Wonsan on 7 December 1950 because of the Chinese attacks but shore installations were destroyed first.

the Yalu and directed him to not allow bombing within five miles of the frontier. MacArthur replied to the Joint Chiefs, whose orders had already been disobeyed, that such bombing was necessary. Washington again gave in to MacArthur's *fait accompli* and merely asked him not to bomb power plants or dams on the river and to refrain from attacking industry in Manchuria across the border. The order was broadened to forbid the bombing of any power plants which supplied electricity to either Manchuria or Siberia. The emboldened general asserted that his weapons were being taken from him.

On 25 October a South Korean force nearing the Yalu was practically wiped out by Chinese troops which seemed to appear from nowhere. Within a few days two Chinese divisions were identified as being in Korea. By 1 November there was no denying it. Communist China had entered the Korean War.

Below: General and Mrs MacArthur at Haneda Air Base, Tokyo on 11 December 1950 when MacArthur returned from a visit to the front in Korea. To the right Colonel Anthony Story, MacArthur's personal pilot, clears the way through the crowds of onlookers.

7:OLD SOLDIERS NEVER DIE...

The Chinese formations, which had moved stealthily across the Yalu, were now beginning to encircle American forward units. Although some of them managed to fight their way out, the situation was serious. MacArthur had grossly miscalculated. These Chinese units were tough, they had excellent commanders and were determined to throw back what they felt to be a dangerous foreign incursion close to their territory. On 1 November Peking Radio announced that operations in North Korea presented a threat to China that they could no longer ignore. Peking asserted that the Chinese people must help North Korea and hurl back the Americans. Despite the fact that MacArthur had already stated that the North Korean army had been destroyed, he was now asking Washington for more men and supplies. What had been more than enough a month before was now inadequate to repel the hordes of Chinese troops that were pouring across the Yalu. MacArthur now had the choice to stand firm, advance or withdraw. He felt that if he continued his advance the Chinese could be stopped. He also believed that it would be impossible to stabilize a line across the top of North Korea because of the terrain and the lack of forces sufficient to establish a position of defense in depth, which would have, he estimated, required three times the number of troops that he had at his disposal. He considered a withdrawal to be contrary to the orders he had been given. He decided to press on and if the Chinese continued to advance, to withdraw swiftly, pulling out the X Corps by sea, thereby exposing the Chinese flank and supply lines to heavy bombing. MacArthur flew to the front on 24 November to watch the final offensive. He noted that the offensive had been delayed over a week due to inadequate supply lines of his own, and despite his and General Walker's fears that American lines were

overextended, he decided to advance regardless.

MacArthur knew that every day brought more Chinese troops across the Yalu, and with a heavy winter close at hand which would freeze the river allowing even more troops to cross easily, it was essential to advance before Chinese superiority on the ground became overwhelming. What he saw at the front discouraged him. South Korean forces were weaker than he expected. He asked his unarmed plane to go forward to the Yalu to inspect the frontier. What he saw was barren countryside, and there was no evidence that a vast army had crossed this wasteland. Nevertheless snow and ice could have covered their tracks, and so MacArthur returned with a conviction that he would wait and see how many Chinese were now in combat before ordering a general retreat. For this action he was awarded the Distinguished Flying Cross by the US Air Force. Upon his return to Tokyo he received word from the Pentagon that decisions were now being made about what course to take next, and in the meanwhile MacArthur should limit his advance in the northeast to Chongjin. Truman was becoming very anxious about a major clash with China which might mean the entry of Russia into the war, based on the 30-year alliance signed between Stalin and Mao in Moscow earlier in the year. By 25 November, the day that Mac-Arthur returned to Tokyo, US Marines had come up to the Chongjin reservoir, and the Eighth Army was slowly advancing – against General Walker's better judgment. The next day the Chinese launched another offensive, led by their commander, General Lin Piao.

The Marines and the Eighth Army were not caught unawares by this assault. Walker told MacArthur that 200,000 Chinese were in the fight, and faced with this overwhelming strength, MacArthur was forced to order a withdrawal which proceeded in good order, fighting all the way. Although the Americans suffered heavy casualties on their march back, it was not a rout, but to regroup somewhere

Left: MacArthur arrives in the US after his recall, flanked by Mayor Elmer Robinson of San Francisco and Governor Earl Warren of California.

along the 38th Parallel required a retreat as swift and complete as the advance northward. Pyongyang was evacuated on 5 December and MacArthur hoped to hold the line.

Meanwhile, MacArthur began a political offensive. He informed the Joint Chiefs that unless the enemy's attention was diverted and his own resources increased it was possible that his forces could be destroyed. This meant that he was encouraging Chiang to attack China from Formosa as a diversionary tactic, albeit with world-wide implications. The Pentagon was struck dumb. MacArthur had disobeyed orders when he sent UN troops up to the Yalu. Would he take precipitate action through Chiang against US government instructions?

At a meeting in the Pentagon a discussion among the Joint Chiefs and the Secretaries of State and Defence took place in which General Matthew B Ridgway suggested to Air Force General Hoyt Vandenberg that MacArthur

Below: Bridges at Sinuiju, North Korea, under attack by aircraft from the USS *Leyte* in November 1950, during the UN retreat from the Yalu.

should be dismissed if he was unable to obey orders. On 5 December Truman issued a directive to all government agencies that no statement on foreign policy be made by anyone without specific clearance from the State Department. He added a second notice admonishing officials overseas, 'including military commanders and diplomatic representatives . . . to refrain from direct communication on military or foreign policy with newspapers, magazines, or other publicity media in the United States.' There was no mistaking this order. Truman had been frightened of MacArthur as the Joint Chiefs had been, but he was not going to stand by while a general in the field directed the foreign policy of the United States. MacArthur's implication that Nationalist Chinese troops be used against the mainland and his explicit request to use them in Korea to bolster the sagging UN defenses was refused. Meanwhile the planned withdrawal of forces from Korea continued, based on directives issued before the Chinese intervention.

MacArthur was totally frustrated. He wanted to win the war in Korea but the US government was denying him both

the tools and the authority to finish the job. Neither the government nor MacArthur was anxious to see a complete defeat for UN forces in Korea, because this would not only imperil Japan but embolden the Chinese and even the Russians to take a more aggressive posture in future crises. With MacArthur suggesting that total defeat was possible unless reinforcements were sent, Acheson and Truman assessed that his judgment on the spot might be correct. Truman realized that MacArthur had disobeyed orders already and that he was threatening to do so again. In his memoirs Truman states that in retrospect he should have fired MacArthur then and there, but he spared MacArthur the indignity at that time because it would have seemed to the public as if MacArthur were being relieved for military failure, which was not the case. Truman said that he did not want to attack the man when he was down. In another statement Truman said that he probably should have fired MacArthur two years before.

MacArthur was defying Truman and this strong-willed President resented it bitterly. He resented MacArthur's popu-

Above: Having retreated below the 38th Parallel, these raiders prepare for defensive action near Yechon, South Korea, on 13 January 1951.

larity at home; he feared his entry into the political scene in America and worse, the strengthening of those forces who were likely to support his viewpoint – not only the Republicans but the radical right of Senators Jenner and McCarthy. The decision to replace MacArthur was almost already made by early December, but the time had to be chosen. MacArthur was wholly unaware of these developments and, far from soft-pedalling, he stepped up his political offensive while his military offensive was rapidly turning into a large-scale retreat. Truman was hoping to avoid all-out war with China – or worse the USSR. Any military buildup in the Far East, Korea notwithstanding, would cut down the military buildup planned for Europe which both Truman and Acheson considered vital to American national defense. Truman had to contend with the attitude of his NATO partners, and in particular Britain.

Attlee asked if he could visit Truman in December. The Labour Party was concerned lest the atomic bomb be used to counteract the Chinese offensive in Korea, a possibility that Truman did not

openly rule out. Attlee arrived in Washington on 4 December. Truman told him that there were few of his advisers who advocated a policy of all-out war against Communist China. He reasserted the position he took with MacArthur at Wake and told Attlee that his orders to MacArthur precluded any unnecessary

Below: LSTs and an LSM carry out the evacuation of Marines from Hungnam in North Korea in December 1950. The retreat continued throughout the month.

provocation of the USSR or of China along their borders. Both agreed that a ceasefire somewhere along the 38th Parallel was the most desirable policy to end the war in Korea as quickly and honorably as possible. They also agreed to try to complete a peace treaty with Japan as quickly as they could and bring Japan into the UN at once as a completely independent state. Thus the underpinnings of MacArthur's power were being cut away from him just as he was intending to launch a major political

offensive in the States against Truman and the Democrats. Truman assured Attlee that he would try to hold the line in South Korea with what troops the UN had and hope for the best. Acheson and Attlee urged Truman not to involve the Nationalist Chinese, as MacArthur had suggested, but that recognition of Communist China should be withheld and Formosa defended against Communist aggression. Thus by the end of the four-day conference Truman had solidified his policy with the British despite some differences which did exist between the two. Both had agreed that the UN should henceforth wage limited war against North Korea and China.

The month of December was a bad one for UN forces. The retreat behind the 38th Parallel continued, but it soon became clear that a defense line could not even be held at that point and would have to be established well to the south. As the military situation worsened, MacArthur began to make his opinions known to Washington. The Joint Chiefs and Truman, based on decisions reached during Attlee's visit, decided that no naval blockade of the Chinese mainland should take place, that no air attacks be made on military and industrial installations in Manchuria, that Nationalist Chinese troops should not be used in Korea, and that no provision for large-scale reinforcement of UN troops in Korea should be made. MacArthur viewed this policy as one of acceptance of complete defeat. He told J Lawton Collins privately (but the information was conveyed to Truman) that he would accept a compromise: a Chinese promise to keep their troops north of the 38th Parallel and UN supervision of a truce. He felt, however, that both these solutions were unlikely, and the alternative of staying on in Korea with the forces he had was impossible. In such an event, he reckoned, the UN would eventually be pushed out of Korea altogether. He also believed that this situation would have a terrible effect on the Western position in Asia generally. The will to resist Communism would be weakened immeasurably.

The Joint Chiefs were polite but firm. They echoed Truman's sentiments that Europe came first and that an engulfment of South Korea by the Communists was preferable to an all-out war with China and the USSR. MacArthur was author-

Above: MacArthur with his eventual successor Lieutenant General Matthew B Ridgway visit the 25th Infantry Division sector on 7 February 1951.

Below: MacArthur and General Walton Walker prepare to meet the press at Wonju during MacArthur's 11th trip to Korea since the start of the conflict.

ized to withdraw to Japan if the situation became hopeless. This was, in effect, a complete reversal of American policy of even a month before, and it came only two months after the US government had authorized MacArthur to send troops north of the 38th Parallel to unite Korea under Syngman Rhee. Why did American policy alter? There are three principal reasons: 1. the November elections were over. A Democratic majority had been maintained and there was no reason to fear a Republican political onslaught immediately. 2. The Chinese had come into the war, making the chances of escalation of the war into a general conflict all the greater and 3. British influence on the American government was brought to bear. Britain had immense interests of a commercial nature in China that it hoped to protect. The British economy was in dire straits; devaluation of the pound had taken place the year before; and Britain was already fighting a guerrilla war against Communist forces in Malaya. It was, of course, in American interests to sustain Britain, who, after all, was the only other power which maintained a large number of troops in occupied West Germany. MacArthur recognized the problem, but he believed that Korea should come first in the light of the Communist threat and that defenses in Western Europe could be built up when the Korean conflict was successfully concluded. He saw the situation in black and white terms. America had an ally in Chiang Kai-shek; why not use his forces, both in Korea and even in mainland China? He suggested this again in a note on 30 December to the Joint Chiefs in reply to their suggestion that he evacuate Korea if conditions became more unfavorable. The request was denied and a series of messages criss-crossed the Pacific as MacArthur sought to change the Pentagon's mind. An impasse had apparently been reached.

In the field the situation worsened, complicated further by the accidental death of General Walker, the Eighth Army commander, on 23 December when his jeep crashed on an icy road in Korea. General Matthew B Ridgway was named as his successor. This placed a man in the field whose loyalty was to the Pentagon and not to MacArthur personally. Acheson considered this to be a blessing in disguise, for here was a man to replace MacArthur if this became necessary and one who would report to the Pentagon if its orders were being countermanded in the field by orders from Tokyo. MacArthur knew that Ridgway was an excellent field commander, however, and he had given him an open brief. 'The Eighth Army is yours, Matt. Do what you think best.'

He ordered the evacuation of Seoul, a further retreat, and the establishment of a new line of defense behind the Han River. A new Communist offensive was

Below: MacArthur inspects a French battalion, attached to the UN Forces near Wonju, on 20 February 1951. This was MacArthur's final visit to Korea.

not expected until after the new year. At this point UN forces numbered about 365,000 while Communist strength was estimated at just under 500,000. Ridgway found the Americans in low spirits but the new commander infused them with new enthusiasm. He felt strong enough to test the enemy's strength in late January and by 9 February 1951 the Eighth Army had fought back to the Han after having withdrawn almost a hundred miles south of it. Ridgway showed that he could drive the Communists back and that MacArthur's dire predictions of total defeat were unfounded.

In late February another offensive carried UN forces to within 50 miles of the 38th Parallel. Seoul was retaken

In testimony of our sincere admiration for our Commander-in-Chief
General of the Army

Douglas MacArthur

His commanders in the field, take deep pride in paying him honor respect and affection upon the occasion of the anniversary of his birthday.

His indomitable courage, resolution and understanding in the face of overwhelming odds in the present Korean conflict, during the course of which we have been privileged to serve under his distinguished leadership, have been a source of continuing inspiration not only to all ranks of the combat elements but also to all freedom loving peoples throughout the world.

That we may meet fully his highest approbation in the test of battle is our sincere hope and determined pledge.

Republic of Korea
26 January 1951

Above: This scroll was presented to General MacArthur on the occasion of his 71st birthday which he celebrated in Korea on 26 January 1951.

Below: MacArthur, Ridgway, Lieutenant Colonel Story, MacArthur's personal pilot, and Major General F W Milburn visit the 25th Infantry Division in early March 1951.

American troops in Western Europe. This debate further clouded the picture in the Far East, for those who were supporting MacArthur's position there were often the same people who were backing Truman on the European issue. Senator Knowland of California, a strong MacArthur man, was behind Truman and his new Supreme Commander in Europe, General Eisenhower, who advocated the funding of a large American contingent in Europe. Senator Taft of Ohio was not so convinced, even though his support of a strong position in the Far East was lukewarm. The linking of the two issues hinged on funding. In December Truman had declared a National Emergency, nominally over Korea, but hoped to use this declaration to bludgeon a reluctant Congress to vote appropriations for the military in Europe. The debate reached its climax in January and funds were finally voted. There was no mistaking the fact that Truman and Acheson, whose main concern was Europe, used Republican interest in supporting MacArthur in Korea to help put the appropriation across. Conscription had been stepped up once the Korean War began, but the draft of civilians into the armed services could only be maintained by a consensus of public opinion.

By now MacArthur's replacement stood high on the list of Pentagon

on 14 March never again to fall into Communist hands. The offensive halted just north of the Parallel by the end of March. Ridgway handled the situation quite differently from Walker. MacArthur had made regular and highly publicized visits to the front in the past which gave the Communists due warning that another attack was at hand. Before the March offensive Ridgway asked MacArthur obliquely not to come this time and MacArthur got the message; he postponed his visit until after the attack was well under way. By this time MacArthur was thinking of a major offensive again to attempt to reunify Korea and totally destroy the Chinese armies in the field. Meanwhile, MacArthur, increasingly out of touch with the impending threat to his position as SCAP and CINCFE, continued his criticisms of the new American policy.

A great debate was raging at the beginning of 1951 about the positioning of

priorities, but again the timing of it was postponed for political reasons. Truman was convinced that MacArthur wished to launch or at least risk a general war over Korea. Truman was adamant that such a risk should not be run and on 14 January sent a personal message to MacArthur restating the position of the US government that the line in Korea should be held if possible but a with-drawal to Japan should take place if necessary. MacArthur repeated his de-sire to attack the 'privileged sanctuary' the Communists had in China and again his request was turned down. He asserted that Chinese aggression could not be stopped merely by killing Chinese (even though the casualty rate for the Com-munist Chinese was staggeringly high by now) and did not want to accept a stalemate.

Upset and frustrated by the intransi-gence of the White House and the Penta-gon, MacArthur took the fateful step of disobeying the President's orders not to make unauthorized statements to the press and contacted Hugh Baillie, President of the United Press, one of America's largest and most influential news agencies. In the message of 15 March he criticized the halting of the Eighth Army's advance at the 38th Parallel short of 'accomplishment of our mission in the unification of Korea.'

Truman and Acheson hoped to ask the Communists to negotiate before US troops went across the Parallel in num-bers again. MacArthur had been in-formed of this move on 20 March and was asked if he could maintain the defense line for a few more weeks until this initiative was followed up. Mac-Arthur replied that he could. MacArthur was determined to undermine the new American policy of stalemate. In a pre-arranged correspondence Congressman Joe Martin of Massachusetts, House Republican Minority Leader, wrote to MacArthur on 8 March informing him that he had urged the use of Nationalist Chinese forces in Korea and that he planned to advocate this view over the radio on 28 March. He therefore wel-comed MacArthur's views on the sub-ject. On 20 March MacArthur replied: 'It seems strangely difficult for some to realize that here in Asia is where the Communist conspirators have elected to make their play for global conquest, and that we have joined the issue thus raised on the battlefield; that here we fight Europe's war with arms while the diplo-mats there still fight it with words; that if we lose the war to Communism in Asia the fall of Europe is inevitable; win it and Europe most probably would avoid war and yet preserve freedom. As you point out, we must win. *There is no substitute for victory*' (author's italics).

Immediately following this message MacArthur asked the Joint Chiefs to lift the military restrictions they had im-posed on his conduct in Korea.

On 24 March MacArthur openly defied the President again by issuing a long public communiqué denigrating Chinese industrial power and offering to meet the enemy Commander in Chief at any time to find a means of solving the Korean dilemma. He claimed that China could be defeated if her coast and interior bases were struck, which would doom the Communist Chinese to military col-lapse. The message was particularly ill-timed. It reached Washington at 2300 hours on the evening of 23 March

Below: General of the Army Douglas MacArthur strides defiantly to his plane, the *Bataan*, which will carry him and his family from Haneda Airbase near Tokyo to the US after his recall on 16 April 1951.

Washington time, and a meeting was hastily convened between Secretary of State Acheson, Alexis Johnson, Dean Rusk and Deputy Secretary of Defense Robert Lovett. The usually imperturbable Lovett was furious and urged that MacArthur be removed at once. The following morning he, Rusk and Acheson were invited to the White House to confer with Truman. Truman's rage was controlled. He sent a terse message back to MacArthur reminding him of the Presidential Order of 6 December and warning him that any further statements by him be coordinated with the Joint Chiefs as prescribed in that order. Truman now believed that he was left with no choice. He could no longer tolerate insubordination by his commander in the field even before the last straw was placed on his back. This took place on 5 April when Republican Congressman Joe Martin read the letter from MacArthur of 20 March on the floor of the House of Representatives. By then Truman had already made up his mind to relieve MacArthur. The reading of the letter to Joe Martin was an open declaration of war by MacArthur on the administration's policy. Furthermore, Ridgway felt that even MacArthur's statement of 24 March made it more difficult to negotiate a peace with the Chinese, 'cut the ground from under the President, enraged our allies, and put the Chinese in the position of suffering a severe loss of face if they so much as accepted a bid to negotiate.' Martin's reading of MacArthur's letter made matters worse for the Administration. If Truman accepted this slap in the face he would have to publicly acknowledge MacArthur's insubordination which had, in fact, been already going on for some time. Furthermore the London *Daily Telegraph* published a dispatch from Hong Kong on 5 April relating an interview MacArthur gave to Lieutenant General H G Martin of the British army. In this interview MacArthur again stated that 'the true object of a commander in war was to destroy the forces opposed to him. But this was not the case in Korea. The situation would be ludicrous if men's lives were not involved.' Senator Homer Ferguson of Michigan then proposed that a congressional committee go out to Tokyo and find out MacArthur's views on how the war should be run. Truman, now exposed publicly at home

and abroad, had no choice but to act and act at once.

On 6 April Truman consulted his senior colleagues. Averill Harriman suggested that MacArthur should have been fired two years before. Secretary of Defense Marshall, possibly remembering his clashes with MacArthur during World War II but valuing his military opinions, advised caution. General Omar Bradley, Eisenhower's close associate in the European war, approached the question entirely from the point of view of military discipline. He saw this as a clear-cut case of insubordination. Ache-

Below: MacArthur and his wife Jean prepare to board the *Bataan* after his dismissal by President Truman and are seen off by members of his staff.

son, a longtime opponent of MacArthur, urged that he be relieved at once, but only if Truman could get the unanimous approval of the Joint Chiefs. He added: 'if you relieve MacArthur, you will have the biggest fight of your Administration.' A Cabinet meeting followed, and although Truman had already made up his mind, he asked for another meeting the following day. By the morning of 7 April Marshall had dug up from the files all the correspondence with MacArthur over the past two years and he told the President that he also now felt that MacArthur should have been relieved two years previously. The Joint Chiefs met on Sunday, 8 April, and on the morning of 9 April there was another meeting of Marshall, Acheson, Bradley, Harriman and Truman. It was the unani-

mous judgment of the Joint Chiefs that MacArthur be removed. That same day orders were issued to that effect and at 1515 hours that afternoon Truman signed them. MacArthur's replacement was also chosen: he was to be Matthew Ridgway.

It was decided that the Secretary of the Army, Frank Pace, should deliver the message of recall to MacArthur in person in Tokyo on the 12th. But late in the evening of 10 April Omar Bradley came rushing over to Blair House, the temporary White House being used by the President while the White House itself was being refurbished. He had heard that a leak of the story of Mac-Arthur's recall was to be made through the notoriously right-wing newspaper, the *Chicago Tribune*, the next day. At this point Truman decided not to give MacArthur the courtesy of the visit by

Frank Pace and simply wire the message of recall to him. A press conference was hurriedly called for one in the morning of 11 April to scoop the *Tribune* and the story was out. Half an hour earlier Truman sent the following message to MacArthur:

'I deeply regret that it becomes my duty as President and Commander in Chief of the United States military forces to replace you as Supreme Commander, Allied Powers; Commander in Chief, United Nations Command; Commander in Chief, Far East; and Commanding General, US Army, Far East. You will turn over your commands, effective at once, to Lieutenant General Matthew B Ridgway. You are authorized to have issued such orders as are necessary to complete desired travel to such place as you select. My reasons for your replacement will be made public concurrently with the delivery to you of the foregoing order.'

Unfortunately MacArthur learned this news second-hand. One of his aides, Colonel Sidney Huff, heard it over the

radio and told Mrs MacArthur over the telephone. MacArthur had just finished lunch and was preparing to leave for the front in Korea. His wife returned to the room where MacArthur and his two guests for luncheon were sitting and told him. When he heard the news, his face froze. 'Jeannie,' he said simply, 'we're going home at last.' After 15 years of service overseas, after 52 years of military service, MacArthur's career was at an end.

The controversy between Truman and MacArthur did not stop with the 1952 election. Certainly Truman's unpopularity as President was never greater than when he fired the General. Although public controversy subsided, more than any other event the firing of MacArthur caused Truman to decide not to run again in 1952, even though he was entitled to do so. The Constitutional Amendment passed during Truman's Administration forbade a President to serve more than two terms, but it was not applicable to the incumbent. Truman has suggested that the decision

Above: MacArthur, his son Arthur and his wife Jean leave the Capitol after he delivered his memorable address to Congress on 19 April 1951.

not to run went back to his inauguration in 1949 and on 16 April 1950, according to his memoirs, he wrote himself a memo stating that he would not be a candidate in 1952. He read this memo to his White House staff when he was in Key West, Florida, in March 1951, just before he fired MacArthur. But by then his mind was made up. He anticipated the public controversy that would ensue after he took the step to fire the five-star general, and his judgment turned out to be right. If he had run in 1952, he would have lost. One of Adlai Stevenson's greatest difficulties during the 1952 campaign was to shake the burden of the Truman Administration, which in good conscience he was unable and basically unwilling to do. Besides he had to run against a great national hero. MacArthur's barnstorming tour in 1951 helped pave the way for Eisenhower; if not one hero, why not another? Thus MacArthur's recall was a crucial issue on which the 1952 election turned.

The Truman-MacArthur controversy has special significance which transcends the political issues of the day. First of all, there can be no question that Truman

did the right thing in firing MacArthur. Whatever the rights and wrongs of the issues which led to his dismissal, no President who hoped to retain democratic government could have failed to act when challenged by a soldier in the field. In the US the President is Commander in Chief of all the armed forces. Therefore, he and the Joint Chiefs were MacArthur's superior officers. Although he was a great soldier, MacArthur forgot the first duty of any soldier: to obey his commanding officer. MacArthur defied his commanding officer time and again; regardless of whether or not Truman was right, he was the President and therefore had to be obeyed. No amount of argument by MacArthur after the event can suppress the fact that MacArthur was allowed quite wrongly, to make policy in Korea as he had done in Japan. In Japan, where MacArthur had the full support of the President, he had developed a talent for self-delusion that was already apparent in him during World War II. He was in Japan and Korea because of the authority vested in him by the President of the United States whose power was given to him by the people through free elections. To defy the President is to defy the expressed will of the people. If MacArthur was allowed to make policy, as, for example, the Japanese military did in the

case of Manchuria and China before World War II, and the Joint Chiefs were content to follow and support it, a drift toward rule by the military in the United States would have inevitably ensued. MacArthur pushed his luck and lost. MacArthur's arrogance could not be tolerated. It was only a matter of political convenience that it was tolerated as long as it was.

The larger issue, however, still remains. Though Truman had to fire MacArthur to maintain constitutional government, was his judgment of the international situation correct? MacArthur consistently supported the view that an all-out war already existed with Communist China as far as Peking was concerned. The US was not fighting to the limit of its capacity, but China was. Therefore, the US had nothing to fear from an all-out war with China since it was already being waged. In retrospect, this indeed appears to be the case. The great danger that the US ran in attacking Chinese territory from the air was the possibility of the Soviets coming to her aid, thereby precipitating a third world war.

Right: Tens of thousands of people welcome MacArthur to the Washington Monument after he told Congress that "Old soldiers never die, they just fade away."

The hindsight that historians are granted leads one to believe that a third world war would not have been considered by the Soviet Union in the 1950–53 period. Although it was not known to the West at the time, Stalin was gravely ill during the later part of this period and he subsequently died in the spring of 1953. A struggle for power then took place within the Kremlin which was only resolved by the emergence of Nikita Khrushchev in 1955–56. This, however, could not be known to any of the principals in the crisis at the time. What was perceived was that although the Soviet Union did have atomic capabilities, it did not have sufficient weapons to wage a successful war against the US. Despite the fact that American armed forces were sorely depleted when the Korean War broke out, the US did have the atomic capability and the means of delivery to lay waste the major cities of the Soviet Union. The USSR did have the ground strength in Europe to cause Truman sleepless nights, but at no time since 1949 has NATO ground strength been capable of hurling back a Soviet attack on the basis of land forces alone. Eisenhower often stated that it was not necessary for NATO to possess this kind of power. The NATO allies relied on supremacy in the air and on the seas.

If the Soviets wanted to launch an attack on Western Europe at any time after 1946, she could have done so, and probably swept to the Rhine at once if not the Channel. It would have meant, of course, that her cities and industrial capacity would have been wiped out. For this reason she did not attack. If domination of any country could be achieved through guerrilla warfare, as in Greece, free elections as in France or Italy, or stealth and intrigue, as in Czechoslovakia, the Soviet Union did not resist the temptation to take advantage of an opportunity. She would not and did not risk general war. The USSR has maintained a Europe-first policy much longer than the United States. Most of the USSR's population and industrial strength lies in the European third of their nation. Although the Soviet Union

Left: Troops present arms to MacArthur and other officials during the service at the Washington Monument marking his official welcome back to the US.

Above: MacArthur addresses the Congress of the United States on 19 April 1951. Vice-President Alben Berkley and Speaker of the House Sam Rayburn sit behind him.

is the largest single land-mass in the world with legitimate interests in the Middle East and in East Asia, her main concern is Europe. One crucial reason for the establishment of puppet governments in Eastern Europe after the war was security for the Soviet population and industrial capacity. There is no evidence to show that Stalin wanted world war at any time from 1945 until his death. After all, he did not invade Yugoslavia when Tito broke with the Kremlin in 1948.

However, despite the fact that Russia sought no world war, an attack on Soviet territory would have given Stalin or indeed any Soviet leader no choice but to respond in kind. MacArthur never advocated an attack on the Soviet Union. He advocated an attack on China's industrial centers in Manchuria and perhaps her coastal cities. Without an attack on the ground in which Chinese territory was penetrated, the USSR is most un-

likely to have gone to war on China's behalf during the Korean conflict. She had already sent arms and advisers, even some pilots, to North Korea, but it is unlikely that she ever considered full-scale intervention. Truman himself proved during the Berlin Blockade that if challenged directly, Stalin would take measures short of war but would go no further. Thus, from a military standpoint, MacArthur was right. Given that the aim of the US and the UN was the unification of North and South Korea, it was worth the risk to try to unify Korea by bombing Manchuria because the risk was slight. This policy was altered by indecision on the part of the Joint Chiefs and Truman, who, after all, vacillated again and again when challenged by MacArthur. They should not have allowed a situation to develop where MacArthur, who had often disobeyed orders, would have to be sacked. Truman did, and therefore he shares the blame for the debacle. MacArthur has quoted Lin Piao, the Chinese Communist general who commanded Chinese troops in Korea, as having stated: 'I would have

never made the attack and risked my men and military reputation if I had not been assured that Washington would restrain General MacArthur from taking adequate retaliatory measures against my lines of supply and communication.' If this quotation is attributed correctly, apparently the Chinese noticed a certain vacillation on Truman's part as well, and acted accordingly.

What of Marshall's and Truman's charge that the US would have lost the support of most of its NATO allies if it had followed MacArthur's advice? Britain was the primary instigator of American fears that she would be abandoned by her new partners in Europe. This was an attitude widely held by the European left, but even socialists in Britain were divided on this point. Subsequent events have proved that even an unpopular war fought by the US in Asia does not wreck NATO. Undoubtedly it affects America's relationship with her allies, but the European members of NATO needed the protection of the United States in the early 1950s more than they do now. They

Above: MacArthur and his family leave the Capitol after he delivered his address to Congress which thrilled his listeners throughout the world.

would have had to swallow, and would have swallowed, all the actions MacArthur put forward because they would have had no choice. Unlike Vietnam, many of the Western European states sent token forces to Korea to placate the Americans. After all, the UN supported the policy of unification of Korea. It was highly unlikely that the NATO allies would have repudiated the US if MacArthur had bombed Manchuria in order to unify Korea.

It is difficult not to draw the conclusion that as MacArthur callously used Korea to bolster his own military reputation as well as an ill-conceived political career in the United States, Truman did much the same thing. Attacked as being 'soft on Communism,' Truman felt obliged to take military action somewhere once Czechoslovakia and China had 'gone down the drain' to Communism. In order to save his own credibility

at home he did not oppose involvement in Korea when it was thrust upon him. It is also possible that he knew what was going on between Rhee and MacArthur and did nothing about it for one very good reason; how else was he going to get Congress to appropriate funds for rearmament, either in Europe or anywhere else? Public sympathy for resisting Communism was already strong in the United States. The American people were reticent about permanent involvement in Europe through a military presence there. It was difficult enough to get the Congress to take the unprecedented act of making an alliance with Europe in peacetime. It would be more difficult to ask the American people to pay for a permanent military machine in peacetime without sufficient cause. Korea provided that dramatic cause which allowed Truman to step up conscription and place the Democrats in a position where they, through Truman, were standing up to the Communist challenge. Once the gesture was made, Truman probably saw that Korea had served its purpose as far as he was concerned. No

need to make MacArthur into a hero once again. Thus, as Roosevelt had used Pearl Harbor to involve the US in the European phase of World War II, Truman very likely used Korea to get America involved in postwar Europe in a significant way. MacArthur, who had done so much for Japan, was used and discarded when convenient by Truman over the Korean issue. This explains the shift in American policy toward reunification of Korea once the 38th Parallel had been crossed.

MacArthur was right on another important count. Military adventures like the Korean conflict are far more easily executed in a totalitarian state than in a democracy. In modern times democracies are forced to conscript civilians to fight their wars. Men will die for simple causes without complaint as long as they, as members of the public at large, are convinced that the cause is just and that lives are not being carelessly thrown away by their military leaders. MacArthur, as a master warrior, saw this point and could not justify losing so many American lives for the sake of

Left: The stalemate in Korea continues as troops of the 45th Infantry Division man trenches ready for action on the front line near Chorwon in early January 1952.

restoring the *status quo* in Korea. You cannot ask mothers to send their boys to be killed for the impotent cause of 'breaking even.' They must, at least at the time, be convinced that they are being asked to make a sacrifice for something greater than themselves, for a cause worth dying for.

The American people enthusiastically supported the Korean involvement because they believed that the liberation of the North Koreans from Communism was such a cause. They believed that Communism was an evil force set on conquering the world. They felt that if aggression was not stopped in Korea, the Communists would go on and on until they were stopped. Better to fight in Korea than in California – this was

Below: Men of the 2nd Infantry Division move out on patrol from their bunker positions at Kumgangsan in early January 1952.

the popular belief. This was not to be an unlimited war on Communism. Conquest of China or the USSR was never seriously contemplated by anyone who held a position of responsibility. It was limited in that its aim was to liberate South Korea and, if possible, North Korea as well. The American people did not want a world war; neither did Truman; neither did MacArthur. What Truman, Acheson and Marshall were eventually content to settle for was a stalemate. MacArthur was not content to settle for a stalemate and was fired for trying to take action to avoid it. Stalemate is exactly what the American people got. The truce line at which the war ended in 1953 after the negotiations at Panmunjom was not dissimilar from the position MacArthur left over two years before when he was relieved of his command. By that time the American people were totally frustrated and glad the war was over. Eisenhower promised to go to Korea to end the war during the last stages of the 1952 election campaign, and many have said that this statement, more than any other, brought him victory at the polls in November. The

American public found the war of stalemate to be futile. It was also immoral. It is wrong to send conscripts out to die for the ignoble cause of breaking even. As MacArthur said, in war 'there is no substitute for victory.' Anything else, especially in a democracy, brings war-weariness initially, then a loss of morale on the part of soldiers and citizens alike, and then bitter resentment and a reluctant conclusion on the part of the people that there is no cause worth fighting for, a conclusion that weakens a nation's resolve to defend its own interests when they are challenged at some point in future. War, as MacArthur knew, is difficult to justify in the best of circumstances. Killing people is wrong and even the most noble of causes cannot make murder right. It can only be justified if the suffering endured by not fighting seems worse than resisting despite the loss of life; if by not fighting today one faces a more difficult and more bloody fight tomorrow. If one is not convinced that it is right to sacrifice men's lives for a cause, then one cannot send civilians to their deaths. MacArthur, the seasoned Warrior of three

Left: Infantry men of the 25th Infantry Division fire a 4.2-inch heavy mortar on Communist hill positions in the Mungdungni Valley in mid-August 1952.

Below: Private Harry Langer of the 25th Infantry Division lights a cigarette after having been relieved from guard on a .30 caliber machine-gun post near Kumhwa in December 1952.

Left: US and ROK MPs interrogate two of the millions of Korean refugees on the road to Taegu, in late August 1950.

great conflicts, realized this. Truman, Acheson and Marshall did not see that their legacy of war without a clear purpose could lead their nation, in another generation, to needless military stalemate in another conflict with disastrous human and ethical results. If you are not sure you are fighting for what is right, do not fight. If you are sure, then no sacrifice is too great.

The American public was shocked, frightened and angry to learn of MacArthur's dismissal. Waves of telegrams and messages of condolence poured into

Below: A wounded scout of the 22nd Infantry Division receives medical attention, while a wounded ROK soldier is helped to this makeshift first-aid station near Kumhwa.

Above: Lieutenant Chung Won, Platoon leader in the 9th ROK Division, briefs his sergeant before going on a mission in May 1953, near the end of the war.

MacArthur's HQ, including one from Premier Yoshida, who credited him with the salvaging of Japan from 'post-surrender confusion and prostration,' thanking him on behalf of the people of Japan for having rebuilt Japan and having planted 'democracy in all segments of our society. No wonder he is looked upon by all our people with the profoundest veneration and affection. I have no words to convey the regret of our nation to see him leave.' Similar letters from Rhee, other high Japanese officials and friends softened the blow. MacArthur prepared to leave for the States at once, where sympathy for him was mingled with rage against Harry Truman, that little Captain from World War I who dared to fire a great national hero.

As soon as the news broke, Joe Martin was out of bed and hard at work on the telephone to both MacArthur and his Republican colleagues in the States. Former President Herbert Hoover, the last Republican to occupy the White House, almost 20 years before, advised MacArthur to fly home 'as quickly as possible before Truman and Marshall and their propagandists can smear you.'

By 10.00 on the morning of 11 April Martin told reporters that after having had a conference with Senator Taft and other Republican leaders it had been decided that there would be a massive Congressional investigation into the foreign policy of the Truman Administration; that MacArthur should be invited to address both houses of Congress; and, 'in addition, the question of possible impeachments was discussed.' The use of the plural implied that not only Truman would be impeached, but Acheson and Marshall as well. On the floor of the Senate Joe McCarthy's partner in red-baiting, William Jenner of Indiana, charged that 'this country today is in the hands of a secret inner coterie which is directed by agents of the Soviet Union. We must cut this whole cancerous conspiracy out of our government at once (public applause from the gallery). Our only course is to impeach President Truman and find out who is the secret invisible government which has so cleverly led our country down the road of destruction.' The Republican Party added to this wave of anger bordering on paranoia to ask if the Truman-Acheson-Marshall triumvirate was planning a 'super-Munich' in Asia. Senator Joseph R McCarthy, in Milwaukee at the time, denounced Truman as 'a sonofabitch' who removed MacArthur when he was drunk on 'bourbon and benedictine.' He

added that if 'Operation Acheson' was not called off, the whole world outside the Western Hemisphere would be lost to Communism and 'Red waters may lap at all of our shores.' Although these statements sound and were extreme, they were not atypical of public reaction at the time. Truman and Acheson were burned in effigy up and down the country and 78,000 telegrams reached the White House, 20 to one against Truman's action. The Gallup Poll reported that only 29 percent supported the President. Despite the fact that most newspapers echoed this national sentiment, the *New York Times* and the *New York Herald Tribune*, probably the two most respected journals in the US, supported the President on constitutional grounds. Truman tried to counter public hysteria by a broadcast on the evening of the 11th. He said that the US was trying to fight a limited war and by doing so, it was preventing a world war – not trying to start one. The broadcast fell on deaf ears. Public sympathy at this point was entirely on the side of the recalled war hero.

In Japan MacArthur's removal generated sincere and deep emotion. He was always almost venerated, his remote and magisterial style appealing to the Japanese people who were grateful to him for all his own sincerity and effort in building up Japan from the ruins of war. The

Above: MacArthur testifies before the Senate Committee investigating Communism in the United States. MacArthur added grist to their mill.

Emperor, who had already written a moving tribute to the General, paid him a visit, the first time in history that a Japanese Emperor called on a foreigner holding no official capacity. Hirohito cried as he said goodbye. This gesture was perhaps the most moving of Mac-Arthur's departure, inasmuch as such a show of emotion on the part of any Japanese is unusual; on the part of the Emperor, unheard of. Between one and two million people lined the roads from the American Embassy to Atsugi airfield, some bowing low, others waving or weeping as his car passed. At the airport he was greeted by a 19-gun salute as Sabre jets and Superfortresses flew overhead. Then, with Colonel Story at the controls, MacArthur's personal Constellation, *Bataan*, took off for the States. It left on 16 April, flew over Mount Fujiyama, and swept eastward toward Honolulu. After a stop at Pearl Harbor, the *Bataan* landed in San Francisco on the evening of the 17th.

The crowds were enormous. It took MacArthur's party almost two hours to travel from the airport to his hotel, despite the fact that he had asked Courtney Whitney to arrange the journey so that he could slip into town unnoticed. The next day, at an official reception at City Hall, he replied to the Mayor of San Francisco by asserting that he had no political aspirations, even though by now his name was being put forward by all sides as a presidential candidate in 1952. He added that 'the only politics I have is contained in a single phrase well known to you – God Bless America.' The roar of approval was deafening. His next stop was Washington. Before he left San Francisco a message came through from the Pentagon that since he was going to address Congress, the speech should be submitted to the Department of the Army. He refused, and the department cancelled the order and apologized. Protocol demanded that he be greeted at the airport by Marshall, Bradley and the Joint Chiefs. Although he arrived after midnight some 20,000 Washingtonians were there to greet him. Greeted by the very men who had brought him down, MacArthur was then mobbed by a frenetic crowd who broke down the crash barriers holding them back. The

President's personal representative, Major General Vaughan, was there too – ironically, since McCarthy had already charged him with crypto-Communism.

The next day, the 19th, he passed more cheering crowds on the way to the Capitol. The tension was considerable, not only among the members of Congress joined to hear his speech, but throughout the country, as tens of millions of people prepared to watch the speech on television or hear it over the radio. At 12.31 MacArthur, in uniform, strode down the aisle to stand at the rostrum in the place usually reserved for heads of state. As the ovation died away he began by stating that he addressed the Congress '. . . with neither rancor nor bitterness in the fading twilight of my life with but one purpose in mind – to serve my country.' He declared that the problem of Communism in Asia and in Europe was the same; that appeasement of Communism in one part of the world will undermine efforts to check its spread in another. Then he confined his argument to a discussion of Asia, which needed to raise its standards of living, not a return to the colonial past. He said that World War II made the entire Pacific Ocean an American strategic frontier, the front line of which was the island chain stretching from the Aleutians to the Marianas. It followed that this line must be held in the name of American national defense. He added that the fall of Formosa to Communism would threaten the Philippines, and the loss of the Philippines and Japan would force the western frontier back to Hawaii or even California, Oregon and Washington. He then went into an apologia for what had happened in Korea. He said that he had never advocated the use of ground forces in mainland China. He said that victory was complete until the Chinese Communists intervened in Korea. He therefore suggested a new policy:

'1. The intensification of our economic blockade of China.

2. The imposition of a naval blockade against the China coast.

3. Removal of restrictions on air reconnaissance of China's coastal area and of Manchuria.

4. Removal of restrictions on the forces of the Republic of China on Formosa with logistic support to contribute to their effective operations against the common enemy.'

MacArthur also claimed that he had asked for reinforcements and had been told that there were none available. He added that if the present circumstances were allowed to continue, the best that could be hoped for in Korea was a stalemate. Rather than being a warmonger, as some had charged him, he said that he hated war and sought its abolition. Once war is forced upon us, '. . . there is no other alternative than to apply every available means to bring it to a swift end. War's very object is victory – not prolonged indecision. In war, indeed, there can be no substitute for victory.' He said that these views had been shared in the past by the Joint Chiefs and practically every leader concerned with the Korean campaign. Constantly interrupted by applause during the 34 minutes of his speech, he concluded his greatest speech by asking, as his soldiers had asked him, 'why . . . surrender military advantages to an enemy in the field. I could not

Below: From left Generals Taylor, MacArthur, Bryan and Garrison Davidson at West Point in 1957. All four served as Superintendants of the US Military Academy at West Point.

answer.' He felt that the argument that China should not be provoked into an all-out war was invalid; so was the fear of a Soviet intervention. 'For China is already engaging with the maximum power it can commit. . . .' He concluded dramatically:
'I am closing my 52 years of military service. When I joined the army even before the turn of the century, it was the fulfillment of all my boyish hopes and dreams. The world has turned over many times since I took the oath on the Plain at West Point, and the hopes and dreams have long since vanished. But I still remember the refrain of one of the most popular barrack ballads of that day which proclaimed most proudly that – "Old soldiers never die, they just fade away." And like the old soldier of that ballad, I now close my military career and just fade away – an old soldier who tried to do his duty as God gave him the light to see that duty. Goodbye.'
There was hardly a dry eye in Congress or in the country. Even those who had opposed him wept openly. In a joint resolution the Congress directed that a gold medal be struck in MacArthur's

honor, bearing the inscription: 'Protector of Australia; Liberator of the Philippines; Conqueror of Japan; Defender of Korea.' Representative Dewey Short of Missouri later exclaimed in the House, 'We heard God speak here today. God in the flesh, the voice of God . . .' Herbert Hoover probably felt this was an exaggeration. He saw MacArthur as 'a reincarnation of St Paul . . . who came out of the East.' That afternoon MacArthur drove down Pennsylvania Avenue as bombers and fighters flew overhead, artillery boomed throughout the Nation's Capitol, and hundreds of thousands cheered him. He was given the freedom of the City of Washington and the day was declared a public holiday.
The next day he came to New York for another parade. At his suite in the Waldorf Towers, which was to be his home for the rest of his life, 20,000 telegrams and 150,000 letters awaited him. Police estimated that 7,500,000 people turned out for the ticker-tape parade, compared with 4,000,000 that Eisenhower got in 1945 when he returned from the war. Crowds were virtually out of control along the 19-mile

route. There was MacArthur, dressed in his trench coat and battered cap, standing almost unseen by the crowd because of the blizzard of paper thrown in his path. People waited for hours to catch a glimpse of this great man. And when he approached, 'There he is,' they shouted, 'There he is!' Some people crossed themselves as his cortege passed. The Department of Sanitation told the story from the amount of paper they collected from the streets: in 1927, at Lindbergh's famous return from Paris after his solo flight across the Atlantic, 1750 tons; MacArthur's return, 3249 tons.

After New York came Chicago, where he addressed 125,000 in Soldier Field on the lakefront; then another great parade to Evanston, north of the city, where he made a short speech in Fountain Square; then on to Milwaukee. It was the same everywhere he went as he toured the country. With each parade enthusiasm slackened ever so slightly. MacArthur correctly discounted the almost religious nature of his progress through the country. It was now more important he thought, to try to follow up his nation-wide triumph with some real political campaigning to put his objections to Truman's policy over to the American people. And it was obvious that his arrival had only begun the great debate.

While MacArthur, having visited the main cities, began to hit the smaller towns – Little Rock, Norfolk, Murfreesboro – arrangements were being made for the Congressional investigations promised by Joe Martin. Between 3 May and 25 June the committee interrogated 13 witnesses, and MacArthur himself was the first to be called to testify. MacArthur was questioned for 22 hours. He repeated his charges that Truman's policy was wrong, but tried to separate Truman and Acheson from the Joint Chiefs, stating, quite incorrectly, that their policy and that of the Administration diverged. In fact, MacArthur had diverged. That was why he was fired. Senator Lyndon Johnson of Texas wanted to know what he would advocate if the Chinese were driven back across the Yalu according to MacArthur's suggestions, but then the Chinese refused to make a peace? The US might then have a limited war with China. MacArthur replied that 'such a contingency is a very hypothetical query. I can't see the possibility of the enemy being driven

Above: Former President Herbert Hoover addresses a crowd gathered at Fort Jay on Governor's Island as MacArthur looks on. Also present, Generals Booth and Bryan.

back across the Yalu and still being in a posture of offensive action.' Would the Soviets intervene, Senator Wayne Morse of Oregon persisted. MacArthur answered: 'My own belief is that what will happen in Korea and Asia will not be the deciding factor in whether the Soviet attacks us or not. If he is determined to attack us, sooner or later he will. . . . I believe the best way to stop any predatory surprise attack by the Soviet Union or any other potential enemy is to bring this war in Korea to a successful end, to impress upon the potential enemy that the power we possess is sufficient if he goes to war to

overpower him. . . .' Earlier he told the committee that if the Korean War was won by the UN, '. . . you will put off the possibility and diminish the possibility of a third world war.' Risk of atomic war with the USSR? Well, MacArthur conceded, the US was 'rather inadequately prepared.' What if the rest of the world didn't support the US in that policy, asked Senator Theodore Green of Rhode Island; then we had better 'go it alone' was MacArthur's reply. As the investigations continued it became apparent that MacArthur was unused to a steady barrage of criticism and that he was unable to match the 'thrust and parry' tactics of political debate. Perhaps he was too straightforward for that. The opposition was well armed. The investigation was a culmination of a rivalry between MacArthur and Marshall which

in its policy from its NATO allies.

MacArthur's denial of disobeying orders does not hold up to any sort of scrutiny and public enthusiasm for him quickly cooled. His half-hearted attempts to run for the Republican Presidential nomination were soon quashed, especially after the less controversial Eisenhower expressed his willingness to run. MacArthur's views on social security, labor unions and other domestic issues were simply too far to the right. Ike said nothing in particular, he was equally as great a war hero, and finally beat Taft to the nomination, although MacArthur was invited to give the keynote address to the Republican Convention in Chicago where Eisenhower was nominated. He was not even invited to the San Francisco Conference later in 1951 which granted Japan her full independence after the peace treaty with her was signed. He was 72 years old in 1952. Often invited to speak about Korea and matters of national security as well as domestic affairs, he almost always accepted, railing against Communists, socialists and corruption in government, but he was increasingly ignored.

Eisenhower met with MacArthur and the designated Secretary of State, John Foster Dulles, a month before he took office and MacArthur made some new suggestions about Korea, including the

possibility of removing all foreign troops from Korean territory, obtaining Soviet agreement to neutralize the peninsula, if such an agreement was possible. MacArthur suggested threatening to clear North Korea of Communist forces and attacking China itself in order to destroy her capacity to wage war. The use of atomic bombs in either operation was not to be ruled out. He again criticized the inertia 'and indecision' concerning the Korean War which he felt the American public was fed up with. Dulles viewed this scenario with some misgivings. But MacArthur replied that Ike could only act boldly in his first three, perhaps six months of office, and after that would just be another politician fighting for his administration. On 16 December 1952 Omar Bradley wrote to MacArthur asking him for his solution to ending the Korean War. MacArthur told Bradley that he would only deal with the President-elect directly but welcomed an invitation to confer with the Joint Chiefs of Staff if they wanted his help. He was never again approached on the subject. He took an advisory executive position as chairman of the Board of Remington Rand and lived with his wife and son, Arthur, in the Waldorf Towers. In effect he just faded away.

Once removed from the field of battle where he was a master and placed in the world of domestic politics, where he was an amateur and out of touch with public attitudes after 15 years of living and fighting abroad, MacArthur's political

Below: MacArthur, followed by General Bryan, inspects the Honor guard at Fort Jay parade ground on 6 November 1957.

had been going on for decades. Marshall put the reasons for MacArthur's recall simply enough:

'What is new and what brought about the necessity for General MacArthur's removal is the wholly unprecedented situation of a local Theater Commander publicly expressing his displeasure at, and his disagreement with, the foreign policy of the United States.'

The points that the Administration brought against MacArthur through the testimony of Bradley and Marshall were twofold: limited war would give the West time to build its strength and in any event, Europe came before Asia; and MacArthur's plan for victory might not end the war even if China was defeated, because the escalation of the conflict might bring about a third world war at a time when the US was separated

Above: Caisson bearing the body of General MacArthur prepares to leave the Capitol in Washington for his burial in Norfolk, Virginia, in April 1964.

fortunes slumped and quickly died. The Eisenhower Administration paid no attention to him, largely because of the attitude of Ike's Secretary of State, John Foster Dulles, who accentuated the coolness already existing between the President and MacArthur. His political pronouncements soon came to and end, and he worked for Remington Rand and lived quietly with Jean and Arthur in the Waldorf. Their suite was a floor away from Herbert Hoover's in the Waldorf Towers, and they often met and talked, two men who had contributed much in their time to their country and who now were all but forgotten.

MacArthur was, perhaps understand-ably, bitter, and often ruminated about the steps that led to his fall. There were, no doubt, many regrets, but he remained unswerving in his belief that there was no substitute for victory in war. He blamed the rise of Communist China in the 1950s, the rape of Tibet and the division of Indo-China on what he called 'the policy of indecision' that brought stalemate in Korea and MacArthur to isolation in the Waldorf. His old age was not without its physical inconveniences. He became ill and suffered a long convalescence, and during this period he often received messages from old friends and comrades from both world wars that cheered him enormously. When he was able to walk outdoors again a passerby stopped him in the street and commented on how much better he looked than in his pictures 'You seem bigger and stronger,' he said, 'and much younger without eyeglasses. Yes, sir,' the man went on, 'your pictures do you a great injustice, Mr Truman.' MacArthur remarked that he didn't know whether to laugh or cry.

In 1961 MacArthur made one last trip to the Far East, a sentimental journey to the Philippines as a guest of that nation on the occasion of the 15th anniversary of its independence. The Manila government declared a national holiday in his honor and a celebration was staged which lasted a week. MacArthur was moved to the point of tears when he learned that his name was still being carried on the company rolls of the Philippine army. When his name was sung out at roll call a master sergeant replied for him, 'Present in spirit!' He visited all the old spots – Corregidor, now covered over by jungle, the hills of Bataan, the beaches of Leyte and the main thoroughfare of

House Speaker, John McCormack, presented it to him and recalled all the past battles in which MacArthur played a role – Meuse-Argonne, St Mihiel, Bataan, Corregidor, New Guinea, Leyte, Lingayen Gulf, Inchon. Hands trembling slightly with age and emotion, MacArthur thanked him and Congress for having offered him this award 'after a lapse of sufficient time to be swayed neither by sentiment nor emotion.'

Soon afterward President Kennedy asked the Treasury Department to mint a special gold medal in honor of MacArthur. On the eve of his 83rd birthday, Kennedy asked MacArthur to perform one last service for his country. American participation in the Olympic Games to be held in Tokyo in 1964 was threatened by a struggle between the US Track and Field Federation and the Amateur Athletic Union over the eligibility of certain American athletes. A similar dispute had taken place before the Olympiad in Amsterdam in 1928 which almost destroyed American participation in the games and MacArthur had settled it. Kennedy asked him to use his prestige as an arbitrator to settle the differences between the two, and MacArthur agreed. The squabble ended in short order.

On 12 May 1962 MacArthur was awarded the Sylvanus Thayer Medal, the highest honor of the US Military Academy. That day he reviewed the Corps of Cadets on the Plain at West Point, lunched with them at the mess, was presented with the medal, and then MacArthur gave an address to the men which was to be his last. He asked the cadets to remember their motto – 'Duty, Honor, Country' – throughout their careers and their lives, which he and his comrades in World War I had held to while '. . . bending under the soggy packs, on many a weary march from dripping dusk to drizzling dawn, slogging ankle deep through the mire of shell-shocked roads, to form grimly for the attack, blue-lipped, covered with sludge and mud, chilled by the wind and the rain, driving home to their objective. . . .' Twenty years later he recalled '. . . the filth of the murky foxholes, the stench of ghostly trenches, the slime of dripping dugouts; those broiling suns of relentless heat, those torrential rains of devastating storm, the loneliness and utter desolation of jungle trails, the bitterness of long separation from those

Luzon, now called the MacArthur Highway. He was told that the world had paid a terrible price when he was prevented from attacking the planes and bases of Communist China at the Yalu. 'If you had been allowed to do your military job there would not have been the disaster of Indo-China; Tibet would not be slave; Laos would not be in the melting-pot; Castro would be an unknown man; and Berlin would not figure so prominently as it does at present.' MacArthur, now an old man of 81, did not respond to this extravagant claim except to reassert the ties of friendship between the US and the Philippines which he had helped to forge. On leaving the Filipinos, for whom he always had a lasting love, always reciprocated, he wistfully told them that 'the burden of the years deems it unlikely that I will, once again, be able to fulfil the vow: I shall return!'

The following year John F Kennedy sent the Presidential jet to New York to bring Douglas MacArthur to the White House. Kennedy had served under MacArthur in the Pacific when he was a PT boat commander during World War II. He knew that MacArthur had always wanted to come to the White House, at least as a visitor if not as a President. Truman, of course, had never invited him. Neither had Eisenhower. Kennedy remarked later that MacArthur warned him, à propos of Vietnam, never to commit a large American contingent to the continent of Asia. His policy had always been, hold firm to the periphery, but never become entangled in long wars in Asia which, for a western nation, can never be won. Both Houses of Congress passed a special resolution expressing 'the thanks and appreciation of the Congress and the American people.'

they loved and cherished, the deadly pestilence of tropical disease, the horror of stricken areas of war; their resolution and determined defense, their swift and sure attack, their indomitable purpose, their complete and decisive victory – always victory – always through the bloody haze of their last reverberating shot, the vision of gaunt, ghastly men reverently following your password of Duty, Honor, Country.' He went on to add that '. . . the soldier, above all other

Below: Statue of General Douglas MacArthur is unveiled at Inchon on 15 September 1957, 7 years to the day after the liberation of the Korean capital.

people, prays for peace, for he must suffer and bear the deepest wounds and scars of war.' He concluded: 'The shadows are lenghtening for me. The twilight is here. My days of old have vanished tone and tint; they have gone glimmering through the dreams of things that were. Their memory is one of wondrous beauty, watered by tears, and coaxed and caressed by the smiles of yesterday. I listen vainly, but with thirsty ear, for the twitching melody of faint bugles blowing reveille, of far drums beating the long roll. In my dreams I hear again the crash of guns, the rattle of musketry, the strange mournful mutter of the battlefield. But in the evening of

my memory, always I come back to West Point. Always there echoes and re-echoes in my ears – Duty, Honor, Country. Today marks my final roll call with you. But I want you to know that when I cross the river my last conscious thoughts will be of the Corps – and the Corps – and the Corps. I bid you farewell.'

General of the Army Douglas MacArthur died in hospital in Washington on 5 April 1964. He was 84 years old. President Johnson ordered the flags to be flown at half-mast. Harry Truman died near his home in Independence, Missouri in December 1972 at the age of 88. His body, and his spirit, outlived MacArthur.